WORDS OF LIFE

THE BIBLE DAY BY DAY
WITH THE SALVATION ARMY

ADVENT EDITION
SEPTEMBER – DECEMBER 1999

GW00640837

Hodder & Stoughton
LONDON SYDNEY AUCKLAND

AND THE SALVATION ARMY

British Library Cataloguing in Publication Data
A record for this book is available from the British Library

ISBN 0 340 72200 2

Typeset by Avon Dataset Ltd, Bidford-on-Avon, Warks

Printed and bound in Great Britain by
Caledonian International Book Manufacturing Ltd, Glasgow

Hodder and Stoughton Ltd
A Division of Hodder Headline PLC
338 Euston Road
London NW1 3BH

Contents

'The Unexpected Grace'

Abbreviations used for Bible Versions

AV	Authorised (King James) Version
GNB	Good News Bible
JB	Jerusalem Bible
JBP	J.B. Phillips – The New Testament in Modern English, 1972 Edition
JM	James Moffatt Bible
LB	Living Bible-Kenneth Taylor
NASB	New American Standard Bible
NEB	New English Bible
NIV	New International Version
NKJV	New King James Version
NRSV	New Revised Standard Version
RAV	Revised Authorised Version
REB	Revised English Bible
RSV	Revised Standard Version

Regular readers of *Words of Life* know that the NIV is the translation used most frequently in these volumes because it is the version most commonly used around the world. Other translations, however, have much merit, not least the translation with which the reader is most familiar. When we concentrate on one passage of Scripture for a time, it would be helpful to use another version and, or, read the passage of Scripture aloud.

Other Abbreviations:

SASB	*The Song Book of The Salvation Army*, 1986
H&H	*Happiness and Harmony* – a supplementary song and chorus book (Salvationist Publishing & Supplies, Ltd.)
WoL	*Words of Life*

All unattributed verse is by the author, Harry Read.

Born to be King

John 18:33–40

'Jesus answered, "You are right in saying I am a king. In fact, for this reason I was born, and for this I came into the world" ' (v. 37b, NIV).

Both new and established readers of *Words of Life* might appreciate an explanation why this Advent Edition should commence with the Passion of our Lord as recorded by John. There are two reasons: first, in the Pentecost volume our progress through John's Gospel brought us to this point and, second, as our key verse indicates, the crucifixion of Jesus, his 'coronation', and acclamation as the triumphant King, were the reasons for his Incarnation. To initiate this volume, therefore, we take up the threads of our Lord's dialogue with Pilate.

Pilate perceived that Jesus was no ordinary king (*v. 33*). It was customary for kings to acquire land, wealth and possessions, and assert authority over people. To enhance and protect their status, they raised armies, built palaces, cities and roads. They silenced opposing voices, laid heavy taxes on their people and ruled as though they had divine authority. It is not surprising that Pilate had difficulty with the Jewish charge that Jesus claimed to be a king. Where were his soldiers, bodyguard, the signs of wealth, his carefully orchestrated public support?

> *He could not see in Christ's humility*
> *The proof of an eternal royalty.*
> *Nor could the Roman Governor understand*
> *True power is in the heart, not in the hand.*
> *Poor Pilate, by his enemies hard-driven*
> *Was not to know Christ is the King of Heaven.*

The values of Christ's Kingdom are so different from the values of our world. We are attracted by the glitter of wealth, the authority to command, the deference given to high rank, the right to occupy a central position on a world stage but *our King came to serve and to die.* Even so, when his work was done he knew that every knee would bow before him (*Phil 2:10*).

PRAYER
> *Lord, Christ, come, dwell within my heart again,*
> *Let your redemption cleanse my every stain,*
> *And come as King, for ever over me to reign.*

No Ordinary Crown

John 19:1–3

'The soldiers twisted together a crown of thorns and put it on his head' (v. 2a, NIV).

Pilate's conduct is held to be consistent with that of a man who was anxious to free his prisoner. He had an instinctive unwillingness to oblige the Jewish authorities (*18:31*), and his wife, in telling him of Jesus's innocence, had warned him against further involvement with the high priest's demands (*Matt 27:19*). It is suggested that Pilate had Jesus flogged in order that the Jews might conclude that this was punishment enough, and that they might be moved to pity. Not for the first time in his governorship of Israel was Pilate proved wrong.

After the flogging, the soldiers, in their rough and dismissive way, mocked him as a king. Some scholars suggest that the crown of thorns was made from the date palm whose thorns can grow to a length of twelve inches; tough and long, each thorn was like a weapon piercing the tender skin of the Son of God. Hundreds of years earlier the prophet Isaiah had given a word-picture of the Messiah in which he indicated that the anointed of God would be humiliated and derided (*Isa 53:1ff.*). The Father knew it was part of the cost of his Son's Saviourhood.

TO PONDER
No ordinary crown our Saviour wore;
No jewel glinted in a band of gold:
Of twisted thorns was made the crown he bore –
The very thought makes loving hearts turn cold.

How dared they to a King by God's decree
Take strong, sharp thorns and make a crown?
Thorns meant by God to save and guard a tree
Now placed on Christ and cruelly pressed down.

We feel the pain of it – we feel the shame
At this mock coronation of our King.
Did Christ not bear God's own most honoured name?
Was this the kind of homage men would bring?

But King he was – this crown a diadem,
Each drop of blood – a love-created gem.

No Ordinary Robe

John 19:1–3

'They clothed him in a purple robe' (v. 2b, NIV).

As we have suspected, with John there is often more significance to his words and his record of events than at first would appear. Behind this account of Pilate questioning the kingship of Jesus and the soldiers dressing Jesus up as a king and mocking him, stands the unspoken irony that the kingship they questioned and mocked was the most valid the world has ever known.

To the soldiers, it was an occasion of coarse, barrack-room humour, the sport of the insensitive, of men part-brutalised by their work. Of all the people they had flogged, not until this day had a 'king' been numbered among them. They could be confident, also, that they would not be censured for their cruel and abusive excesses. After the crown had been pressed on Christ's noble brow they took a robe, probably long-discarded by an officer, draped it around Jesus in recognition of his 'majesty' and subjected him to further indignity and pain. For *them* it was light relief in the course of a long, hard day – for *him* it was part of the price of his role as Redeemer (*cf. Isa 53:3*).

We visualise the scene – an old purple robe flung dramatically across the bleeding form of Heaven's King – we hear the taunts and sounds of the uncouth merriment of hardened men, and he who could have used his enormous power to stop them chose instead to accept in silence (*cf. Isa 53:7*) this dehumanising preparation for his crucifixion. What a great Saviour we have!

TO PONDER   *They put a soldier's robe around the Christ –*
   Messiah, Son of God and Prince of Peace
Who, in that cause would soon be sacrificed
   That soldiers' duties everywhere might cease.

And when they scorned his kingship, struck his face,
   Another error these poor soldiers made:
He was, and is, the King of love and grace:
   A King to hear, a King to be obeyed.

The soldiers thought their victim but a fool,
They did not know that he had come to rule.

No Ordinary Judgment

John 19:1–4

'Once more Pilate came out and said to the Jews, "Look, I am bringing him out to you to let you know that I find no basis for a charge against him" ' (v. 4, NIV).

Although it was early morning and Pilate, irritated by the Jewish leaders but aware of their power over him, delivered a judgment on Jesus which was clear and unbiased: there was no basis for a charge against him. Modern translations bring out the legal aspect of Pilate's words more than the less precise but still true, older version, 'I find no fault in him' (*AV*).

If Pilate had possessed the insights needed, he would have been able to say that Jesus was not only blameless in the eyes of the law, but that in every way he was without fault. In his own way, the Roman governor was trying to free Jesus from the hands of his enemies. Had he been a lesser man, he would not have tried – had he been a bigger man he would have succeeded because he would not have been open to blackmail by his enemies.

In one of our Lord's confrontations with his opponents he challenged them, 'Can any of you prove me guilty of sin?' (*8:46*). They were unable to do so, of course. It will be remembered also that, in order to make a charge against him, false witnesses had to be sought (*Matt 26:59*). In our times, when it is almost standard practice for politicians and the media to ferret out and publicise the follies of opponents or other high-profile people, it is significant that our Lord's enemies, who must have initiated their own enquiries, could find no sin in him. We can only conclude that the sinlessness of Jesus emphasises the eternal quality of his life and reinforces his claim to be the Son of God. It was the time of the Passover and, even as Pilate spoke, lambs without blemish (*Exod 12:3 AV*) were being prepared for sacrifice and Jesus, the Passover Lamb without blemish or defect (*1 Pet 1:19*), was also being prepared.

TO PONDER   *The holy, meek, unspotted Lamb,*
Who from the Father's bosom came,
Who died for me, e'en me to atone,
Now for my Lord and God I own.

(*Nicolaus Ludwig von Zinzendorf,*
trs John Wesley, SASB 116)

A Test of Mercy

Luke 14:1–5

'One Sabbath, when Jesus went to eat in the house of a prominent Pharisee, he was being carefully watched. There in front of him was a man suffering from dropsy' (vv. 1,2, NIV).

For our Sunday readings we turn again to our Lord's parables as Luke recorded them. The setting for these parables was the home of a prominent Pharisee to which Jesus had obviously been invited for a meal. Luke made the comment that Jesus was being 'carefully watched', a fact which warns us that the invitation was more calculating than sincere. With a complete lack of subtlety, the Pharisees had placed a very sick man in a central position. Jesus had only two alternatives: he could either heal the sick man or ignore him. If he ignored him, he had failed the test of mercy and, if he healed him, he had failed to honour the law regarding the Sabbath. Clearly, the watching Pharisees believed they had placed Jesus in a 'no win' situation.

With great wisdom, Jesus asked the Pharisees a simple, highly relevant question, 'Is it lawful to heal on the Sabbath or not?' (*v.* 3). We note that they remained silent (*v.* 4). Had they answered 'yes' they would have been guilty of breaking the petty laws they considered to be so important; on the other hand, had they said 'no' they would have revealed their carelessness of a sick man's pitiable condition. Nevertheless, although on the Sabbath, as on other days, they took care of their animals (*v.* 5; *cf.* 13:15), they were unwilling to take care of sick people.

Jesus took hold of the man, healed him, and sent him on his way. Our Lord may have failed the legal test, but he passed the test of mercy. F.W. Farrar commented wisely, 'As though the reception of divine grace were Sabbath-breaking toil!'

TO PONDER

The law of mercy supersedes
Conventional and formal law;
A human being's obvious needs
Should cause the coldest heart to thaw.
The Christ, who is of love and grace the sum,
Would have us each more merciful become.

PRAYER SUBJECT

For more families to become Christian.

No Ordinary Man (1)

John 19:1–5

'Then Jesus came out, wearing the crown of thorns and the purple robe. And Pilate said to them, "Behold the Man!" ' (v. 5, NKJV).

'Beauty' says the proverb, 'is in the eye of the beholder' and, if that is so, we wonder what those who beheld Jesus, Son of God and Son of Man, saw on that fateful morning when Pilate presented him to them. Did they see him as pretender to the ancient throne of Israel? An aspirant to the honoured role of Israel's Messiah? Or as a highly-gifted man whose fantasies had run away with him and who had now received his just reward? We try to imagine the crowd's reactions to this man who was clad in a mock robe of royalty, crowned with a painful wreath of thorns, his body lacerated and bleeding from the whip and his face bruised and swollen by the soldier's fists. 'This man', they may have been saying to themselves, 'could be neither king nor Messiah; had those roles been his destiny, God would never have allowed this shameful event to take place.'

Some people had thought earlier that Jesus was John the Baptist or Elijah, Jeremiah or another of the prophets (*Matt 16:14*), but not now. To them, the Sanhedrin had proved Jesus to be a blasphemer and the soldiers had turned him into a figure of humiliation. The Messianic bubble had burst. The dream was broken. The pretender was exposed. What good could come out of Nazareth anyway (*cf. 1:46*)? In spite of all his fine words and deeds, he was still only a man. The crowd passed judgment on Jesus and, in so doing, passed judgment on themselves. Without realising it, their superficial judgment was to blight their lives.

Throughout history, people have beheld this man and many have dismissed him as 'merely a man'. They have considered his claims to be preposterous and have excluded him from their lives. Many have used his name as a swear-word; others have lampooned his person. They have judged him thus and, in doing so, have misjudged him and are lesser people because of it.

PRAYER

> We pray for those who cannot see
> Christ came, a king to set us free,
> And that he reigns in majesty,
> O'er earth and o'er eternity.

No Ordinary Man (2)

John 19:1–5

'Then Jesus came out, wearing the crown of thorns and the purple robe. And Pilate said to them, "Behold the Man!" ' (v. 5, NKJV).

Because there is so much truth in the proverb, 'Beauty is in the eye of the beholder' (*WoL 6 Sept 99*), we who love our Lord see him not as the bleeding victim of rough and uncouth soldiers, nor as a pawn in a game being played by the Roman governor, nor even as a tragic focus of priestly fear and hate. We see him as Son of God and Son of Man – the Redeemer of the world.

In Pilate's invitation to look at Christ we hear also the overtones of wonder that God's Son would even become a man and, becoming a man, accept such humiliation in order that we might be delivered from all we have allowed ourselves to become. The tone of Pilate's invitation is more accurately translated by 'Here is the man!' (*v. 5 NIV cf. JM*) Pilate's voice expressed a measure of scorn as he directed attention to the pathetic sight of an already cruelly beaten man. He did this so that the Jews might see the improbability of Jesus being a king, and their feelings of pity would enable Pilate to set him free. To us, however, as we behold him, there is nothing pathetic about him. We see him draining sin's cup of bitterness on our behalf (*18:11b*). He is our hero – our deliverer – our Saviour. More than anything else, we want to serve him, love him, be like him.

We see him as the Word made flesh (*1:14*), who freely took on the weaknesses of the human race (*Phil 2:7*) and bore in his body and on his heart the pain, shame and weight of human sin (*cf. 2 Cor 5:21; Isa 53:3–7*). Our gaze takes us past what the soldiers did to him to what he has done for us and, in consequence, our hearts are full of love for him. His wounds, cruelly inflicted and voluntarily born, are precious because we know that there is no limit to his love for us. Thank you, Lord!

PRAISE *Behold the Man – and we the Christ behold.*
  We see his wounds, we see his thorn-crowned brow,
 And as we gaze on him our hearts are told
  Salvation is not only then – but now.
 He was, and is, and always will be King,
 Whose glory was revealed through suffering.

A Spontaneous Reaction

John 19:1–6

'As soon and the chief priests and their officials saw him, they shouted, "Crucify! Crucify!" ' (v. 6a, NIV).

Once again Pilate had miscalculated. When he presented Jesus to those who had charged him with aspiring to the throne of Israel, instead of a wave of sympathy moving towards our Lord because he had been ill-treated and was clearly guiltless of the charge, Pilate was greeted with the cry, 'Crucify! Crucify!' The men who made that terrible demand were devoid of compassion: they illustrated the tragedy of a loveless religion.

The sense of tragedy is heightened because the religion of the Jews was based upon the compassion which God had for them as a people. He loved them and, loving them, had initiated their release from Egypt. The same love is reflected in the prophet's words, 'How gladly would I treat you like sons . . . I thought you would call me "Father" ' (*Jer 3:19*), and is made even more clear with, 'I have loved you with an everlasting love; I have drawn you with loving-kindness' (*Jer 31:3*). God intended them to love him totally and to love their neighbours as themselves (*Deut 6:4,5; Lev 19:18; cf. Mark 12:30,31*). Their religion, however, had been emptied of love and had been replaced by a rigid formalism which culminated in the demand, 'Crucify'.

There have been times when the Christian faith has forgotten its obligation to show the Master's compassion. The Crusades, from the first millennium onwards, followed by the Inquisition to root out heresy, were not noted for compassion. Christian slave-owners often displayed more ruthlessness than love; and do we not have terrorist groups today who claim to be acting in the name of God? A loveless religion is often the ground in which cruelty flourishes, which explains why men who should have known better could look at Jesus and cry, 'Crucify!'

TO PONDER

> *The men of God cried, 'Crucify!'*
> *When they beheld God's only Son.*
> *Their hate decreed that he should die,*
> *And hate, it seemed, this war had won.*
> *But hate could never conquer love,*
> *As Calvary was soon to prove.*

A Surrendered Responsibility

John 19:1–6

'But Pilate answered, "You take him and crucify him. As for me, I find no basis for a charge against him" ' (v. 6b, NIV).

Throughout this trial we become aware of Pilate's exasperation with the Jewish leaders. Their Jewishness, as revealed through their laws on ceremonial cleanliness (*18:28*), their persistence, their hatred of Rome and the fact that they were in a position to affect his future (*cf. v. 12 with Luke 13:1*) must have been a constant irritation to him. Presumably, these factors conspired to make Pilate lose patience and, after his attempts to release Jesus failed, to say, 'You take him and crucify him' (*v. 6b*).

As we read the tragic account of Pilate's surrender to the priests we can hardly avoid the comment that 'it is not possible to evade our personal responsibility towards Jesus'. Each one of us is accountable for our reactions to him. Matthew records that Pilate called for water and washed his hands symbolically in front of the people, declaring his own innocence in Jesus's death, putting the responsibility on them (*Matt 27:24*). If he thought that his ploy was successful, the judgment of history is that he failed. For centuries the creed has carried the statement, 'Suffered under Pontius Pilate'; it is a declaration in history people ignore to their peril, because we cannot evade responsibility for our responses to Jesus.

If Pilate shrugged off his responsibilities in the interests of political expediency it achieved very little. His term of office was soon ended following complaints made against him by the Samaritans. Pilate stands condemned, also, for his moral failure; he knew what was right and made the wrong decision. He knew Jesus was innocent of the charges made against him, but allowed him to fall into the hands of his enemies and die by crucifixion. For this, history will always condemn him.

TO PONDER

> *We take responsibility*
> *For how we handle Christ.*
> *Do we accept his Saviourhood*
> *Or is he once more sacrificed?*
> *His kingly claims we never must ignore*
> *Because he reigns in Heaven for evermore.*

A False Assumption

John 19:1–6

'But Pilate answered, "You take him and crucify him' (v. 6b, NIV).

Pilate was having a very bad day! It had started all too early and the Jewish leaders were all too persistent and Jesus, the man they wanted to kill, was enormously impressive. Instead of helping Pilate as she thought, his wife had disturbed him further by warning him not to 'have anything to do with that innocent man'. (*Matt 27:19*). We speculate whether Pilate, governor of a small Roman colony, accepted with philosophic resignation the fact that occasionally governors had difficult problems to face, and considered them as 'all part of a day's work'!

If Pilate believed that this problem of Jesus could be solved by a politically-based decision, he was making a false assumption. Jesus has never been one of life's *incidental* issues. He is not even a *major* issue. He is *the supreme* issue of life. What we do with him determines everything we do in life: other issues and questions fade when compared with the Lordship of Jesus and the questions he poses. The 'Jesus issue' never goes away. Pilate discovered that and so have we. The entire world will discover it in time. On that fateful Friday there was the death of Jesus which comforted his enemies and, no doubt, gave Pilate some relief. But there was a Resurrection, an Ascension and, in due course, there was the gift of the Holy Spirit.

When the Spirit came he was to convict the world of sin and to reveal Jesus (*16:8–15*): quite clearly, there is no escape from the 'Jesus issue'! Furthermore, because God has decreed that we are accountable for our actions, a Day of Judgment has been planned (*Matt 16:27; Acts 17:31*), and Scripture makes it clear that the judge whom God has appointed is none other than the Christ (*5:22*). To those who have made the right decision concerning him that is a comforting and reassuring fact.

PRAYER   *Lord, help me see the worth of Christ to me,*
          To let him reign supreme within my soul;
          And let my life so much more Christlike be
          As daily I submit to his control.
          Let all I am acknowledge Calvary's claim,
          And all I do bring honour to his name.

Pilate's Dilemma

John 19:1–6

'But Pilate answered, "You take him and crucify him. As for me, I find no basis for a charge against him" ' (v. 6b, NIV).

Although Pilate was in the process of surrendering Jesus to the Jewish leaders (*WoL 9,10 Sept 99*) he reaffirmed his position concerning our Lord's innocence (*18:38*). Probably because their first charge, that Jesus claimed to be the King of the Jews, had appeared to fail, they revealed the real cause for their opposition. This reason was not political but religious, and it related to his claim to be the Son of God (*v. 7*). First stated in John's Gospel by John the Baptist (*1:34*), the theme recurs (*3:18; 10:36; 11:27*), as does his claim to be at one with the Father (*10:37,38; 14:10*). Indeed, so much of John's Gospel affirms Christ's unique relationship with the Father that we begin to understand why unspiritual men who occupied leadership positions wanted to destroy him, and why they pointed to the law which authorised their action (*Lev 24:16*).

During his governorship Pilate had demonstrated his insensitivity to the Jewish religion, but he became fearful when he heard that Jesus had claimed to be the Son of God (*v. 8*). To understand his fear we have to remember that he was a widely travelled Roman who was used to the idea of many gods. He probably believed many of the myths that were in circulation, including the stories of gods who visited earth (*cf. Acts 14:8–18*), some of whom, according to ancient belief, had sons by ordinary women, and the sons, being half-man and half-god, were unbelievably strong. By pagan standards, Pilate had much to fear.

If Pilate was inclined to set Jesus free earlier, he was more determined to do so now (*18:38*). He had been responsible for the flogging and humiliation of 'the Son of God' (*v. 1*) and he may well have wondered how much worse his day could become.

PRAYER

Because Christ is the Son of God
   His love and grace surround me,
I will not fear upon my road
   Though in the past fear bound me.
Those myths of long past, darkened days
Are lost in Christ's enlightened ways.

A Test of Humility

Luke 14:7–11 (following Sunday 5.9.99)

'For everyone who exalts himself will be humbled, and he who humbles himself will be exalted' (v. 11, NIV).

If the Pharisees were watching Jesus (*v. 1*), he was watching them also (*v. 7*). The difference between their watching, however, and his, was that they were hoping to see him embarrassed and discredited, whereas he watched in order to help. As with every such occasion, the seating arrangements at the dining tables meant that some guests would be better placed than others. The places of honour (*v. 8*) were either near to the host, or where the conversation was most likely to flow. Jesus noticed how eagerly, even aggressively, some guests claimed the best places, and he commented accordingly.

On the one hand, our Lord's advice that people should choose the lesser places and give opportunity for advancement, rather than choose the greater and expose oneself to humiliation (*vv. 8–10*), was practical advice. To be asked to move down is a blow to self-esteem and such blows can be painful, whereas to move up enhances self-worth and status. On the other hand, our Lord's words on humility have a spiritual significance.

Humility was a strong characteristic of our Lord. He humbled himself and because of that self-humbling God exalted him and gave him 'the name that is above every name' (*Phil 2:8,9*). Jesus encouraged everyone to 'learn from me, for I am gentle and humble in heart' (*Matt 11:29*). Seeking the highest places is a failure in love insofar as we devalue other people in the exaltation of ourselves. In his prologue to those great verses on the humility of Jesus Paul said, 'Do nothing out of selfish ambition or vain conceit, but in humility consider others better than yourselves' (*Phil 2:3*). It is good advice.

PRAYER

Lord, help me to enhance another,
  Not by self-demeaning thoughts and ways
But, valuing him, as though a brother,
  Worthy of respect, and love, and praise.
Let me, Lord, in true humility
Show this side of Christ's divinity.

PRAYER SUBJECT *For Christian voices to be heard in government.*

A Perceptive Question

John 19:7–10

'And he went back inside the palace. "Where do you come from?" he asked Jesus' (v. 9a, NIV).

From the inscription Pilate later ordered should be placed at the top of the cross, we deduce that Pilate knew Jesus was from Nazareth, that unfashionable and ill-regarded town from the north (*2:46; WoL 21 April 98*). As a place name it would be of little significance to Pilate: it could have been Capernaum, Tiberias or Megiddo for all he cared. The place name, however, rooted Jesus geographically but now, driven by fear, Pilate looked beyond Nazareth to wherever was Christ's true source of origin, and asked, 'Where do you come from?' Perhaps, in this moment, Pilate remembered Christ's answer to an earlier question about his kingship, 'My kingdom is not of this world' (*18:36*) and began to worry about what he had done to Jesus.

Our Lord had impressed Pilate as a non-threatening person, but 'Son of God'? (*v. 7*) That had sinister overtones for the governor: son of a Roman god? a Greek god? a local deity? Was Jesus the son of a god of war, of peace or of pleasure? Pilate was fearful (*v. 8*), and rightly so, because his safety was at stake.

If Pilate's finger had been more sensitively on the pulse of the nation he might have known more about the claims of Jesus. It is difficult to imagine that in such a small country crowds in their thousands could assemble to listen to a religious radical without questions being raised in the governor's palace. During his ministry Jesus had supplied information concerning his true beginnings. He claimed a life with God, the Father, that pre-dated Abraham (*8:54–58*), and that he had been sent by God (*cf. 8:16–29*). He claimed also, 'I and the Father are one' and that he was 'God's Son' (*10:30,36*). Nazareth was important only as the place of Christ's upbringing. If only Pilate had the mind to know the place from whence Christ actually came!

PRAYER
It was from heaven the Saviour came,
*   To rescue us from all our shame.*
He came the Father's love to show
*   And then, with him to Heaven go.*
The glories of that place we cannot see,
But Heaven with Christ is where we want to be.

A Silent Response

John 19:7–10

'And he went back inside the palace. "Where do you come from?" he asked Jesus, but Jesus gave him no answer' (v. 9, NIV).

An ordinary man facing crucifixion would not have remained silent when his judge asked him a question. Fear of that dreadful punishment would, surely, unlock any tongue – any tongue that is, except the tongue of our Lord, because he had nothing to say to Pilate that could help him in those brief moments. If Pilate had failed to understand the kind of king Jesus was, if he had failed to wait for an answer when Jesus referred to truth and Pilate replied, 'What is truth?' (*18:36–38*), then this was not the time to launch into an exposition of God's purposes behind Christ's Incarnation. We note other occasions when Jesus remained silent. Matthew and Mark record that Jesus was silent before the high priest; silent also when the Jewish leaders listed the charges they were making against him to Pilate (*Matt 26:63; 27:14; Mark 14:61; 15:5*) and, according to Luke's record of Jesus before Herod, Jesus remained silent there (*Luke 23:9*).

We make the assumption that the silence of Jesus was a judgment against his accusers. Had he been able to say something at that time to help them, we can be sure he would have said it. But, we surmise, he knew their minds were set. They had looked at the Son of God, the noblest man the world has ever known, and had proceeded to treat him shamefully (*cf. Matt 12:22–32*).

Since Pilate began to be 'even more afraid' (*v. 8*) when he learned that our Lord had claimed to be the Son of God (*v. 7*), he might have been wise to be even more fearful than ever at the silence of Jesus. It is serious, indeed, when a man's attitudes are so ingrained that Jesus stands before him silently. How glad we are of prayer and a sensitive spirit that enables us to share fellowship with the Lord of life!

PRAYER

> *Talk with me, Lord, thyself reveal,*
> *While here o'er earth I rove;*
> *Speak to my heart and let me feel*
> *The kindling of thy love.*

(*Charles Wesley, SASB 636*)

Power (1)

John 19:7–10

' "Do you refuse to speak to me?" Pilate said. "Don't you realise I have power either to free you or to crucify you?" ' (v. 10, NIV).

Pilate was quite right: he did have power to set Jesus free or to crucify him, because as the representative of the Emperor very substantial powers had been vested in him. It is true that the power was not absolute insofar as if he overstepped the mark he could be called to account and punished severely, but, so far as his prisoner was concerned, he had the power to free and the power to crucify.

One of the amazing things about God is that he grants freedom to each one of us to take whatever action we please against himself and his Son. We have the freedom to choose or reject, to adore or to abhor, to praise or to blaspheme. Presumably, because of Christian values the world's media is at best tolerant of Christ and his people, and at worst goes far beyond the bounds ordinary fair-minded people would consider reasonable, as they lampoon Christ and ridicule his people. Even so, the response of the Master is predictable: no lightning bolts of judgment descend from heaven; no outraged God cries 'enough is enough'. Freedom means freedom; except, of course, that our freedom has eternal consequences, and what we do with Jesus determines our lives now and in eternity (*WoL 9 Sept 99*).

Judas was free to betray his Master and Peter was free to deny him. The high priests were free to fabricate charges against him and Pilate was free to hand him over for crucifixion. By the same freedom, however, Peter was able to repent and serve Christ faithfully to the end of his days, as were all those who, drawn by Jesus, committed themselves to him. That same freedom is ours: we are free to live for him, die for him if necessary, but always to bring glory to his name.

PRAYER

> *My freedom, Master, let me use*
> *Your will to find, your way to choose;*
> *And through my freedom let me be*
> *Of all things wrong an enemy.*
> *Let me not make a dubious choice,*
> *But choose to make your heart rejoice.*

Power (2)

John 19:8–11

'Jesus answered, "You would have no power over me if it were not given to you from above" ' (v. 11a, NIV).

Although Jesus remained silent when the governor asked him where he had come from (*v. 9*), he spoke with great directness when Pilate asked further, 'Do you refuse to speak to me? ... Don't you realise I have power either to free you or to crucify you?' (*v. 10*). Jesus rebuked the man of power with, 'You would have no power over me if it were not given to you from above.'

Two important issues are implicit in our Lord's statement. In the first place, it is assumed that God intended that people would be governed and that power was available to those who were placed in positions of authority (*cf. Rom 13:1*). Christians should obey the properly constituted means of government. It will be recalled that Jesus had already laid down the all-important rule, 'Give to Caesar what is Caesar's and to God what is God's' (*Matt 22:21b*). There is a realm which, by God's ordering, belongs to the civic authorities, and God intends that Christians should be law-abiding; indeed, Christians should be the best citizens of all (*cf. Titus 3:1; 1 Pet 2:13–17*).

This counsel raises the challenge of what Christians are supposed to do when they are subject to evil rulers. Throughout the centuries and, even today, Christians are facing this problem with wisdom and courage. Clearly, God would not expect us to honour an evil government by suggesting that those who worked evil did so at his command, although he is not slow to bring good out of such evil. A gross misuse of power does not have his blessing, and Christians must use the wisdom God gives them to decide how they respond. Jesus was, however, making it clear to Pilate that, although he claimed power, it was his only because God, as part of a general strategy, had planned it that way.

PRAYER
> We pray, O Lord, for those who live
> Where evil men exert their power.
> We ask that you will wisdom give
> And grace, to live each testing hour.
> Remind them, Lord, that we who freedom share,
> Through you, are bound to them in faith and prayer.

The Mystery of Pilate's Power

John 19:7–11

'Jesus answered, "You would have no power over me if it were not
given to you from above" ' (v. 11a, NIV).

Although the power referred to (*v. 10b*) was the civil power Pilate wielded
as the representative of Caesar, there was more to it than that because he
was dealing with Christ. An added and mysterious factor was that the
events which led to Christ's crucifixion can hardly be judged as being out
of control. God's hand on the proceedings is apparent and Christ's
sufferings were voluntarily borne (*WoL 7 Sept 99*). He *could* have walked
away from the soldiers, the Sanhedrin and Pilate; he *could* have come
down from the cross (*cf. Mark 15:29–32*) but chose not to do so. Jesus
knew he was to die on the cross; he knew he was the Passover Lamb,
slain for our sins (*1 Cor 5:7*), the 'Lamb slain from the creation of the
world' (*Rev 13:8*).

What we know of God makes it difficult for us to believe that he
ordained that Judas should betray Jesus (*cf. 6:70*), that Caiaphas should
deliver him up to Pilate, and that Pilate should *surrender him* up for
crucifixion. These things, however, happened, and there is evidence
enough to suggest that crucifixion was always in God's mind. How, for
instance, can Psalm 22:1–18 be interpreted other than by a crucifixion –
the crucifixion? Scholars tell us that the Psalm perfectly describes how a
victim felt (*Ps 22:14–17*), and Isaiah's prophecy (*Isa 52:12–53:12*), in
Christian thinking, can refer only to a suffering Saviour.

Even though Judas, Caiaphas and Pilate were not ordained to their
tasks – had they been ordained they could hardly have been guilty – God
knew that there were men who, by their freely made choices, had become
men of *that* kind, and they became willing partners in those events which
led to the redemptive death of Jesus on the cross. It is a mystery to us
how men, by their own free choice of evil, could become part of the
divine plan to save the world from its sinfulness, but it happened.

PRAYER   *Our finite minds can never understand*
              The mysteries of your power, your grace and love;
              But how we thank you, Lord, that you have planned
              To save us; your power to show and love to prove.

The Greater Sin

John 19:7–11

'Therefore the one who handed me over to you is guilty of a greater sin' (v. 11b, NIV).

On balance it would appear that 'the one' to whom Jesus was referring was Caiaphas, although it could be argued that Jesus was referring to Judas. Technically, however, Judas handed Jesus to the high priest and it was the high priest who handed Jesus over to Pilate. Our key verse, therefore, makes it clear that Caiaphas and Pilate are guilty men but that Caiaphas was guilty of the greater sin (*for Judas see Matt 26:24*). All three men were guilty of the sin of unbelief (*3:18*) from which other sins spring: not least, that of betraying the Son of God.

By his heritage and training Caiaphas should have been looking forward to the coming of the promised Messiah. His prayers, worship in the synagogue and Temple, reading of the Scriptures and contact with some of the best minds of his day should have prepared him for Christ's coming. Instead, Caiaphas allowed himself to be ensnared by power and materialism. His peers were the family into which he had married (*18:13*), the family who had turned the 'Father's house into a market!' (*2:16*). It was then that God entered more obviously into the struggle for the soul of Judaism; but Caiaphas and his like were determined men.

Caiaphas had refused to enter Pilate's palace lest he should be defiled and be made unfit to share the Passover Feast of thanksgiving to God (*18:28*). In imagination we see him standing outside the palace inciting the crowd to demand the death of Jesus, the only Son of the God of the Passover. It is one of our Lord's maxims that, 'from everyone who has been given much, much will be demanded' (*Luke 12:48; WoL 29 Aug 99*) and Caiaphas, given so much, had failed. His less privileged background meant that Pilate's sin, though great, was less than that of the priest.

PRAYER

So much, Lord, you have given me
    Of faith and of your love and grace.
Let my accountability
    To you be true as life I face.
O, make me strong and sensitive
To combat wrong and for you live.

Immediate and Long-term Gains

Luke 14:12–14 (following Sunday 12.9.99)

'Then Jesus said to his host, "When you give a luncheon or dinner, do not invite your friends, your brothers or relatives, or your rich neighbours; if you do, they may invite you back and so you will be repaid" ' (v. 12, NIV).

It was not discourtesy but concern that made Jesus address a direct word to his host on the subject of invited guests. With the exception of the sick man whom he cured (*vv. 1–4*), whose presence reflected the cynicism of the Pharisee, Jesus could see that everyone present had been chosen from the Pharisee's peers to attend the meal. In fact, they were an elitist, exclusive group of like-minded people who gave support and encouragement to each other. As Jesus was to point out later, his Kingdom was inclusive, not least of the poor and deprived (*vv. 21–24; 15:7*).

Those people who want an immediate reward can invite friends, relatives and the rich and, in all probability, this will result in them becoming guests of their guests. As Jesus commented, 'so you will be repaid' (*v. 12b*). Those, however, who stand nearer to God will see the plight of the needy and distressed, the outcasts and social misfits and will have compassion on them. They will invite them to a banquet and, by so doing, will be blessed (*v. 14a*). Experience confirms that when we do good works we always feel blessed – there is an immediate blessing; but Jesus had in mind the reward which will come at the day of judgment (*v. 14b*). On that great day the superficial things of life will be seen for what they are, and those deeds that have been done in the Master's name will reap an enormous reward. To stand before the judge with empty hands because we disregarded God's perfect way for us and chose immediate rather than long-term rewards, could be a very salutary experience indeed.

TO PONDER   *I seek the blessing from the Lord*
                 That humble saints receive,
             And righteousness, his own reward
                 To all who dare believe.
                         (William Drake Pennick, SASB 461)

PRAYER SUBJECT   *Impoverished and dispossessed people.*

Pulled Both Ways

John 19:7–12

'From then on, Pilate tried to set Jesus free, but the Jews kept shouting, "If you let this man go, you are no friend of Caesar. Anyone who claims to be a king opposes Caesar" ' (v. 12, NIV).

Pilate could have claimed that he was the free man and that Jesus was the prisoner, but he would have been wrong. Although bound, Jesus was free to follow his destiny, whereas Pilate was a prisoner to his past. Following our Lord's words on power, the governor seemed to be persuaded that he was a visionary and not a threat to Rome, hence the desire to release Jesus. But Pilate's enemies were too strong for him. As B.F. Westcott said, 'Pilate [had] to choose between yielding to an indefinite sense of reverence and right, and escaping the danger of a plausible accusation at Rome.' With such a clear choice before him, Pilate was prepared to make the political decision and surrender Jesus to the mob, but would taunt them in the process (*v. 14b*).

Most of us are familiar with the dynamics of mob behaviour. Television cameras have occasionally shown us a large group of reasonably well-behaved people suddenly become irrational and violent. Normal thought and restraint are abandoned as the will of a small group of fanatics spreads with amazing speed across the group, and explodes with frightening effect. Some of those who became part of the mob clamouring for the death of Jesus might well have been among those who had been blessed by his ministry but now, Jesus the friend had become Jesus the enemy.

If Pilate had been a man of acknowledged integrity it would not have been possible for these determined men to blackmail him. Pilate knew, however, as they knew, that an official complaint to Caesar, to the effect that he had spared the life of a man who had kingly aims in the city of Jerusalem, would mean that Rome would deal with him swiftly and ruthlessly.

PRAYER *'When I want to do good' said Paul,*
'Evil is right there with me' (Rom 7:21)
A fact that is true of us all
Till Christ grants us liberty.
Our numerous sins may before us be massed,
But he breaks the chains and the power of the past.

The Final Presentation

John 19:12–14

'When Pilate heard this, he brought Jesus out and sat down on the judge's seat at a place known as the Stone pavement' (v. 13, NIV).

We are told that the words 'kept shouting' (*v. 12*) come from a Greek word which actually means, 'yelled or screamed'. William Temple implies that these harsher words are not used in English translations because they are 'out of harmony with the dignity of the narrative'. The clamour was loud enough, not only to penetrate the palace walls, but to convince Pilate that he had failed. So he brought Jesus out again to face his enemies. Because the original Greek allows of two interpretations, scholars are a little divided as to whether Pilate himself sat on the judge's seat or whether he sat the thorn-crowned Christ on it (*cf. v. 13 JM*). Dramatically, the second option is stronger, insofar: as it presents Jesus in the seat of power and gives Pilate freedom to assert himself over the baying crowd as he said, with a measure of contempt, 'Here is your king' (*v. 14*).

John times this moment at about 6am on the morning of the Day of Preparation of Passover Week (*v. 14*): that is to say, Friday. There were some present who had not slept for twenty-four hours because of their involvement in the capture and trial of Jesus and there was much still to be done. Christ had to be crucified, die and be buried; they had to share in the Passover meal and then they could rest. With the death of Christ they could conclude that it had been worth the loss of a little sleep, and they could rest more easily in their beds.

God times this day as the day in human history when his plan for the forgiveness of the world's sin was achieved. To this day everything from creation had been looking forward, and everything since that day looks back. In the Father's timing, the Passover Lamb was to be slain – the King was here to reign.

PRAYER
'Here is your king' the feeble governor said,
  But they saw not a king in Jesus Christ;
They saw the crown of thorns around his head,
  And then demanded he be sacrificed.
They were so blind; they simply could not see
That crown but added to his majesty.

A Pause for Reflection

John 19:13–15

'But they shouted, "Take him away! Take him away! Crucify him!" '
(v. 15a, NIV).

As we try to visualise the dreadful scene of a bruised, bleeding, thorn-crowned Christ being presented to the crowd as their king, our hearts feel the pain of their rejection of him. We hear their frenzied cries of, 'Take him away – crucify him' and hold the scene in our minds in order to reflect on this unjust and incredible moment in world history. He was the Christ who had come to save his people (*Matt 1:21*), who had ministered with great tenderness and compassion to their physical and spiritual needs. 'Come to me,' he had said, 'all you who are weary and burdened, and I will give you rest' (*Matt 11:28*), and they came in their thousands because 'the common people heard him gladly' (*Mark 12:37 NKJV*). He gave hope to all who knew they were needy: the lepers, the blind and those described as sick; he loved all people and gave the children a special worth (*Luke 18:15–17*); and he wept over Jerusalem (*Luke 19:41–44*).

Even so, the crowd – which may have included some of those who had been blessed by his ministry – led by the frustrated and frenzied priests was demanding that Jesus should be taken away. They were insisting not merely that he be removed from sight and denied his ministry among them, but that he should be taken away and crucified! Could they really do that to him?

Jesus knew that they could – and would! He knew the prophecies related to himself (*Luke 4:16–21*), and had he not recently told the story of the tenants in the vineyard and their treatment of the master's son? (*Luke 20:9–19*) Soon he would be opening the Scriptures to the two disciples on the Emmaus Road and later to the whole group (*Luke 24:25–27, 44–46*). Evil had to show its hideous strength in order that he might conquer it.

To PONDER *How could men look on Christ with so much hate –*
His claims rejected be, his love denied;
His capture and his flogging celebrate,
And then demand that he be crucified?
How could he yield to their unjust demands,
Except he yielded first to love's commands?

An Interesting Question

John 19:13–16

' "Shall I crucify your king?" Pilate asked' (v. 15b, NIV).

Pilate's awareness of the power given to him by Rome overwhelmed our Lord's words to him, 'You would have no power over me if it were not given to you from above' (*v. 11a*), hence his question to the waiting Jews, '*Shall I . . .*'. They would feel the sting in his words because they knew that Pilate was indulging his contempt for them, but that they were prepared to accept, so long as he submitted to their demand for the death of Jesus. Pilate's question, however, is worth further thought.

'Shall I crucify your king?' asked Pilate; and throughout the long history of our faith many people have confessed that, in a mystical though real way, they did, and do still, help to crucify him. The Holy Spirit has his own way of interpreting the death of Jesus to us, making us realise that it has a personal application over and above its historical significance. Those who were present at the death of Jesus were witnesses to an act of eternal consequence: that is to say, an act that would never lose its meaning, power or relevance. Part of the Holy Spirit's ministry to us is to work within our hearts to make us know, and feel, that our sins – my sins – continue to drive in the nails, thereby crucifying the Christ afresh (*cf. Heb 6:6*).

> Ah, holy Jesus, how hast thou offended,
> That man to judge thee hath in hate pretended?
> By foes derided, by thine own rejected,
>   O most afflicted.
>
> Who was the guilty? Who brought this upon thee?
> Alas, my treason, Jesus hath undone thee.
> 'Twas I, Lord Jesus, I it was denied thee:
>   I crucified thee.
>
> For me, kind Jesus, was thy incarnation,
> Thy mortal sorrow, and thy life's oblation;
> Thy death of anguish and thy bitter passion,
>   For my salvation.

                              (*Robert Bridges*, based on *Johann Heerman*)

An Inconceivable Repudiation

John 19:13–16

' "We have no king but Caesar," the chief priests an – swered'
(v. 15c, NIV).

Israel was intended to be a theocracy, that is to say, a nation ruled not by kings but by God (*cf. Exod 19:5–8; Num 9:18; Deut 29:9–15*). God exercised his will through chosen men but, it will be recalled, how reluctantly he indulged the Israelites in their demand for a king (*1 Sam 8:4–22*). It is a matter of biblical record that the kings were subservient to God (*1 Sam 13:13,14; 2 Sam 12:1–25*). The Jewish expectations of the Messiah included the belief that he would reign over them as king – a king of the house of David (*Isa 9:7; Jer 23:5*). Nathanael would be typical of those devout Jews who were looking for the Messiah and, when he met Jesus he said, 'Rabbi, you are the Son of God; you are the King of Israel' (*1:49*). The roles of Messiah and King were closely linked in the expectations of Israel.

Of the many references to our Lord's kingship in the New Testament we select only his triumphal entry into Jerusalem. He who came in the name of the Lord was the rightful King of Israel (*12:12–15*). Jewish history also shows how the people, with enormous courage and initiative, resisted and rebelled against the rule of foreign kings, including the Roman Emperor.

When the chief priests responded to Pilate's contemptuous question, 'Shall I crucify your king?' and they replied, 'We have no king but Caesar', they were going against their history, their Messianic expectations and God himself. It was a blasphemy of enormous proportions. D.A. Carson commented, 'Their repudiation of Jesus in the name of a pretended loyalty to the emperor entailed their repudiation of the promise of the kingdom of God'. As John so rightly observed in the prologue to his Gospel, 'He [Jesus] came to that which was his own, but his own did not receive him' (*1:11*). It was a great tragedy.

PRAYER   *In these events we see what hate can do,*
                   How hate can close the mind and blind the eyes;
              But, Lord, we also see how love shines through,
                   And those who know you are by love made wise.
              All hateful thoughts in me eradicate,
              And all your plans for me, Lord, consummate.

Satisfaction

John 19:12–16a

**'Then at last, to satisfy them, he handed Jesus over to be crucified'
(v. 16a, REB).**

One event can satisfy different people in different ways. The chief priests were satisfied that the governor had yielded to their pressure and Jesus would die. They would also be grateful for the fact that they would be able to participate in the Passover meal. It had looked as if Pilate was going to delay things by making difficulties, but his surrender was just in time.

Although Pilate was unhappy because a man he considered innocent was going to be executed, he could console himself that life was cheap and Jesus would not be the last innocent man to die. The chief priests, however, who had been hinting that they would report him to Caesar, had actually declared publicly, 'We have no king but Caesar' (*v. 15b*). That statement satisfied Pilate and, if Caesar heard of it, he would be satisfied as well.

Dare we presume to suggest that Jesus was satisfied? Not at the terrible sights and sounds of evil to which he had been exposed in the past hours, of course, but satisfied because he was at one with the Father's will and in loving obedience was about to take his cross and die for the sins of the world. Did not Isaiah say of him, 'He shall see of the travail of his soul, and shall be satisfied' (*Isa 53:11 AV*)? And for precisely the same reason, was not God, the Father of us all, satisfied?

From that day to this, and it will be so to the end of time, men and women who have found salvation through the sacrifice of Jesus for sins, have been satisfied with the forgiveness they have received. That forgiveness would have been sufficient of itself to bring satisfaction but he who gave his life continues to do so and we, the redeemed, have the remarkably fulfilling experience of sharing the Resurrection life of Jesus.

TO PONDER

> *And O, that he fulfilled may see*
> *The travail of his soul in me,*
> *And with his work contented be,*
> *As I with my dear Saviour.*

(*Dora Greenwell*)

A Spontaneous Reaction

Luke 14:15 (following Sunday 19.9.99)

' "Blessed is the man who will eat at the feast in the kingdom of God" ' (v. 15, NIV).

Scholars interpret our key verse differently. There are those who think it was the reaction of a traditional Jew who believed that only those regarded as the sons of Abraham (*cf. John 8:33*) will be seated at the banquet table of the Messiah. Those scholars discern in the statement the complacency of chosenness. Because God had chosen Abraham and by birth they were Abraham's descendants, they were privileged and secure, whereas the unchosen Gentiles were lost. The lostness of the Gentiles was not even sad to them; it was just the way God had decreed.

There are other commentators who read a different message in this guest's exclamation. To them, this man had recognised the kingdom Jesus was representing. He saw through the cynicism of his host in confronting Jesus with a very sick man (*v. 2*) and acknowledged the divine nature of Christ's healing power and wisdom (*vv. 3–6*). When the Master pointed out the shallowness of their pride in seeking the best places at the table (*vv. 7–11*), this unidentified guest could only concur and, as Jesus indicated the exclusivism inherent in their system of hospitality, he knew that their system was wrong. He knew, also, instinctively and with certainty, that the God who had rescued the Hebrew slaves in Egypt had not lost interest in others similarly distressed. Furthermore, by the words and actions of Jesus, this man had become convinced that the word God gave to Abraham that all the world would be blessed through him, was true (*Gen 12:3b*). We share the assumptions of the scholars who think this way, and believe that the guest's statement was one of hope in the unfolding purposes of Almighty God.

PRAYER

> *Break through my reservations, Lord,*
> *   The barriers I have made;*
> *Let me receive the Saviour's word,*
> *   His truth my heart persuade.*
> *Let me, who am of saints the least,*
> *Be present at that heavenly feast.*

PRAYER SUBJECT   *Christians who work with disadvantaged children.*

David and Absalom

2 Samuel 13:30–38 (following 3.7.99)

'The king stood up, tore his clothes and lay down on the ground; and all his servants stood by with their clothes torn' (v. 31, NIV).

We continue with the story of David, Israel's most famous king, who was still living under the shadow of his affair with Bathsheba and the murder of her husband, Uriah (*11:1ff.; WoL 17–22 June 99*). Nathan's prophecy that 'the sword shall never depart from your house, because you despised me and took the wife of Uriah the Hittite to be your own' (*12:10*) was in the process of coming true. Because of Amnon's sin against Tamar (*vv. 1–22*), Absalom, charming, persuasive, ambitious and unforgiving, arranged the murder of Amnon, his older brother (*vv. 23–29*). By so doing he avenged his sister's honour, but he removed also the brother who stood between himself and the right of succession to David's throne. We make the assumption that the ambitious and unforgiving Absalom would be happy on both counts.

At first, David was told that Absalom had killed all his sons, and he was inconsolable in his grief (*vv. 30,31*). Jonadab, David's nephew, tried to give balance to the situation by assuring David that only Amnon was dead (*v. 32*). This was the same Jonadab who had advised Amnon concerning Tamar and who, in a sense, was a principal cause of the problem (*vv. 3–6*). With shrewd, self-interested people like Jonadab in the king's court, trouble of one kind or another was unavoidable.

The arrival of the watchman confirmed the truth of Jonadab's words. Only Amnon was dead, and Absalom had fled to stay with his mother's family (*v. 37; cf. 3:3b*). Possibly, the time spent in his grandfather's court served only to strengthen Absalom's ambitions, and give him time to devise ways whereby he might win over the people of Israel (*cf. 15:1–12*). David, however, was left to mourn the death of one son and the exile of another.

PRAYER
The pain of loss is hard to bear,
The pain of mourning hard to share;
So deeply personal is grief,
So difficult to find relief,
Except that Christ, who always feels our pain,
His comfort gives; again, and yet again.

Difficult Days

2 Samuel 14:1–20

'Joab son of Zeruiah knew that the king's heart longed for Absalom' (v. 1, NIV).

Joab was a faithful servant of David and he had concerns both for the king and for the nation. He knew that the king loved Absalom, as our key verse says: he 'longed for Absalom' and, as a servant and friend, Joab wanted to ease the pain in his master's heart. The other serious factor related to the need for the royal succession to be re-established. Amnon, the brother slain by Absalom, had been the acknowledged crown prince and David had not replaced him. Although it seems unthinkable that a man should gain a crown through murder, Absalom's revenge had conveniently placed him as the first in line for the throne. Absalom's personal popularity (*cf. v. 25*) meant that the people would not have objected to his becoming the crown prince, and many people would have thought he had served them and the honour of Tamar well by ridding them of the unworthy Amnon.

In order to achieve these objectives Joab resorted to the kind of subterfuge Nathan the prophet had used to good effect on an earlier occasion (*12:1–14*). Tekoa was located some five miles from Jerusalem and Joab sent there for a 'wise woman' whom he probably knew. This 'wise woman' had to be more than just wise: she had to be a convincing actor (*vv. 5–8*), nimble-witted enough to press for more than the king first gave her (*vv. 9–11*), courageous enough to put a direct challenge to him (*vv. 13–18*), and diplomatic enough to keep the good relationship between Joab and David intact (*vv. 19–21*). Joab had chosen well and the woman was a total success.

Perhaps we should observe that, in spite of David's sense of loss and an element of instability in the kingdom, he fulfilled his duties faithfully. As king and judge, he remained accessible to his people, giving them all the time they needed.

TO PONDER
*Sometimes, when heavy burdens press
And hearts are sore through deep distress,
When most events feel out of joint
And common duties lose their point,
It's then we need God's special grace
To live life at our normal pace.*

A Partial Reconciliation

2 Samuel 14:21–24

'The king said to Joab, "Very well, I will do it. Go, bring back the young man Absalom"' (v. 21, NIV).

We do not know if David was reluctant to receive his son Absalom back from voluntary exile. Certainly, his heart would be glad (*cf. v. 1*); but if he took no disciplinary action against Absalom, his presence in Jerusalem would constantly rebuke his failure to do so. Perhaps David suspected also that his wilful and ambitious son would exploit his weakness at the first opportunity. It would have been a well-founded suspicion.

At a distance of three thousand years from the events we are considering, it is relatively easy to pass judgment on David. We must remember also that we have the benefit of our Lord's teaching, and two thousand years of the Holy Spirit's work in establishing standards. In considering David's behaviour, however, not in a spirit of judgment but in order to learn from it, we would probably be right in assuming that his affair with Bathsheba had not only reduced his credibility as king and zest for good government, but had increased his insecurity. At this important stage in his rule he lacked wisdom and, perhaps more importantly, the wisdom to seek guidance.

Help in decision-making is not hard to secure and for the king it was probably easier than for others. David had Joab available, but his wisdom was of the 'street-wise' variety. Ahithophel was David's official counsellor (*15:12*) and he, no doubt, could have been helpful. He had also the prophet Nathan who could have shared his own special insights. Above all, he had God to whom he could turn. But the unsatisfactory way in which Absalom was brought back to the country and left to his own devices seems to suggest that David had an uncertain touch on events and these developed to the disadvantage of everyone.

PRAYER
    I need wisdom, Lord,
      I cannot trust in common sense
    When there are facts I do not know.
      From out your great omniscience
    Help me the right decision, Lord, to make,
    My way to close, your chosen way to take.

A Simulated Reconciliation

2 Samuel 14:25–33

'Then the king summoned Absalom, and he came in and bowed with his face to the ground before the king. And the king kissed Absalom' (v. 33b, NIV).

It is hard to use generous adjectives to describe Absalom. He was extremely vain (*v. 26*), full of self-justification and wilful in the extreme. Anyone else who had murdered a brother would have considered an unpunished return to Jerusalem to be an act of unmerited benevolence on the part of the man who was both his king and father. Alas, Absalom did not even have the grace to consider himself guilty of wrongdoing (*v. 32b*).

Obviously irritated and affronted by the fact that he had been two years in Jerusalem and his father, the king, had not sent for him, Absalom decided on his own strategy. Since he was back home because of the intervention of Joab (*vv. 19–23*), it was to Joab he turned. We do not know why Joab refused further involvement with the isolated prince but, petulantly and arrogantly, Absalom ordered his servants to set fire to Joab's barley crop (*v. 30*). In a dry climate, the results of such action could have been calamitous, but that meant nothing to Absalom. His tactics were successful: Joab visited him and agreed to see the king on his behalf (*v. 33a*). As a result, David sent for Absalom, who bowed before his father, the king, and a reconciliation was effected. Because of David's love for Absalom (*18:33*), the reconciliation was real on his part, but Absalom had no love for his father and, for the son, the reconciliation was just another part of his plan to become king of Israel.

Our word 'hypocrite' comes from the Greek word for actor. The acting profession is honourable, but play-acting in relationships is not, as our use of the word 'hypocrite' indicates. All our relationships should be based on openness and integrity.

TO PONDER
> *For words without the heart*
> *The Lord will never hear;*
> *Nor will he to those lips attend*
> *Whose prayers are not sincere.*

(John Burton, jun, SASB 588)

The Real Absalom Emerges

2 Samuel 15:1–6

'He stole the hearts of the men of Israel' (v. 6b, NIV).

Sooner or later Absalom's ambition required him to make a move against his father and, blatantly but skilfully, he began to woo his father's followers with such success that the historian was able to record, 'he stole the hearts of the men of Israel'. He obviously capitalised on his appearance (14:25,26) and the impact his presence achieved. Clearly, Absalom looked every inch a king. Standing in his horse-drawn chariot, moving no faster than the speed of the fifty men who ran ahead of him, he must have cut an attractive, dramatic figure (v. 1). We are left to assume that he also exploited the weakness of his ageing father and the gullibility of the people.

Perhaps David's court no longer opened at the early hour his subjects would have liked but by standing at the approach to the city the regal, energetic figure of Absalom must have contrasted sharply with that of his father. Not many would consider his words to be wrongfully disloyal to his father (vv. 2–4), especially if they had to wait some time before the older man was available for consultation and decision-making. Furthermore, Absalom's treatment of the men who bowed before him made them feel that they stood in a special relationship to him. Honoured and flattered, they gave their hearts to this arch-manipulator.

It is difficult to imagine that David had not been made aware of Absalom's activities. Fifty impressively mobilised runners are not easily concealed. The same location, frequently used for the same purpose on a main road, could not go unnoticed and people would talk – how they would talk! David must have been informed and seems to have done nothing. Was he wearying of the intrigue? the demands of leadership? or did he just think that all of Absalom's manoeuvres would come to naught?

TO PONDER
A moment comes when something must be done,
Inaction has not many battles won;
Not every problem can be solved by time,
'One stitch,' the proverb wisely runs, 'saves nine.'
We have the Counsellor to be our guide,
With all we need of wisdom to provide.

A Mistaken Sign

2 Samuel 15:7–9

'At the end of four years, Absalom said to the king, "Let me go to Hebron and fulfil a vow I made to the LORD" ' (v. 7, NIV).

The vow which Absalom made while living in Geshur was: 'If the LORD takes me back to Jerusalem, I will worship the LORD in Hebron' (v. 8). We visualise Absalom, in voluntary exile because he had murdered his brother Amnon (13:28,37), living comfortably in the palace of his maternal grandfather (3:3b), and dreaming of his future role as king of Israel. Not surprisingly, in his ambitious and ruthless mind emerged the thought that if ever he returned to Jerusalem it would be a sign that he was to be king of Israel. Absalom probably chose Hebron because it was inside Judea; it had been the city where David was twice crowned (2:4; 5:3), and its people might have been resentful at its loss of status when David made Jerusalem the capital city. As a centre from which to start a rebellion, Hebron was ideal.

Absalom, therefore, interpreted Joab's intervention on his behalf (14:1–24) as a providential sign – and he was wrong. He had failed to understand the immediate past history of the kingship. Only two men had been king of Israel and both had been anointed by a prophet (1 Sam 10:1; 16:12,13). What made him think that God would allow a self-appointed king?

He had failed, also, to understand the God in whose name he claimed to be acting. Had he not observed how God had punished David for his sins against Bathsheba and Uriah (12:1–14)? Absalom had murdered, dishonoured his father and coveted his father's kingdom (cf. Exod 20:12,13,17). God could not honour him. Lastly, Absalom had failed to understand his own heart. He had the heart of a manipulator, an avenger and despot – qualities God opposed. Absalom may have had the people with him (v. 13), but God was not with him. He would, therefore, fail.

TO PONDER   *If God himself our ways oppose,*
The victory lies with all our foes.
Regardless of our strength and skill,
We cannot force on God our will.
Though dreams of glory we might entertain,
Should God not honoured be – our dreams are vain.

A Gracious Invitation

Luke 14:15–24 (following Sunday 26.9.99)

> **'Jesus replied: "A certain man was preparing a great banquet and invited many guests" '** (v. 16, NIV).

It will be remembered that Jesus was a guest in the home of a prominent Pharisee where, regardless of the fact that it was the Sabbath, he had healed a sick man (*vv. 1–6*), and had proceeded to give advice on the subjects of humility and hospitality (*vv. 7–14*). Taking the cue from a guest who had exclaimed, 'Blessed is the man who will eat at the feast in the kingdom of God' (*v. 15*), our Lord told this parable of the great banquet.

We note that many guests had already been invited and, in the prevailing culture, the host had every right to expect them to come when they were called. Not only would the host expect those who were invited to come, but all who received the invitation would expect to be present. It was customary for servants to be sent to the guests telling them that the feast was ready (*v. 17; cf. Matt 22:1–4*) but these guests, instead of preparing themselves and attending the feast, sent excuses only (*vv. 18–20*).

The 'certain man' in the parable was God himself and the banquet of which Jesus told was the feast of the kingdom of God which all Jews, as the offspring of Abraham, expected to attend. Hence the spontaneous comment made by one of the guests (*v. 15*). But Jesus knew the laws of the kingdom better than his hearers who had closed their hearts to those laws. They had closed their hearts to him also, and in closing their hearts to him, they had closed their hearts to the *Father* (*John 8:42–47*). Jesus elsewhere stated the problem in the bluntest of terms: 'He who hates me hates my Father as well' (*John 15:23*). As people relate to the Son, so they relate to the Father.

PRAISE

Come, sinners, to the gospel feast,
Let every soul be Jesus' guest;
Ye need not one be left behind,
For God hath bidden all mankind.

(Charles Wesley, SASB 234)

PRAYER SUBJECT　　　*The work of evangelism in our local churches.*

Thorough Preparation

2 Samuel 15:7–12

'The conspiracy gained strength, and Absalom's following kept on increasing' (v. 12c, NIV).

Absalom's cunning, patience and thoroughness paid him rich dividends. By the simple expedient of ingratiating himself with the people who had legitimate complaints for the king to handle (*vv. 1–7*), he assured himself of growing support in the country. Somehow, he had won also the support of Ahithophel, David's most trusted counsellor (*vv. 12b,31*). He had organised his communication system so that the whole nation would know at the same time that he had been proclaimed king (*v. 10*) and had succeeded in keeping word of his activities from reaching his father (*v. 9*). In addition to that, most shrewdly he had arranged for two hundred highly influential people to accompany him to Hebron. They were unaware of his intentions (*v. 11*) but their presence gave the impression of support for his rebellion. As hostages, these men could have been of great value to Absalom insofar as pressure might well have been exerted on their families in Jerusalem, had David decided to defend the city.

Any religious fears the Jews might have had were allayed because Absalom astutely made sacrifices to God (*v. 12a*). Again, however, Absalom's disregard for history is evident: when Saul offered sacrifices instead of leaving that ritual to the prophet, it marked the beginning of the end of his reign (*1 Sam 15:13–35*). Absalom was shrewd, but not shrewd enough.

Sin has a blindness all its own. Although the record does not set out to define Absalom as a fool, the facts add up to that. We deduce from this that anyone who attempts to build, either without God, or in defiance of him, is doomed to failure.

PRAYER

> *Nothing can I achieve, nothing attain;*
> *He that without thee builds, labours in vain;*
> > *Shatter my own design,*
> > *Shaping a plan divine,*
> > *Come to this heart of mine,*
> > > *Saviour, again.*

(John Gowans, SASB 605)

An Encouraging Loyalty

2 Samuel 15:13–22

'Ittai replied to the king, "As surely as the LORD lives, and as my lord the king lives, wherever my lord the king may be, whether it means life or death, there will your servant be" ' (v. 21, NIV).

When David learned that Absalom had won the hearts of the people he assumed that his son had proclaimed himself king (*cf. v. 19*). His keen military mind told him also that Absalom would waste no time in attacking Jerusalem and David knew he had neither the time, nor the men, to defend the now-vulnerable city; wisely, therefore, he ordered its evacuation (*v. 14*). Happily, those who were near to David were utterly loyal to him, including the foreign mercenaries who formed his body-guard.

The conversation with Ittai, the Gittite, who led the mercenaries, must have encouraged him. Ittai was a Philistine – a Gittite is a man from Gath – and many a man similarly placed would have accepted the advice not to become involved in a civil war, but Ittai was different. His reply, which included the statement, 'As surely as the LORD lives' (*vv. 21a*), seems to suggest that he had converted to Judaism, and his assurance of loyalty revealed his respect and admiration for David as both king and person. For David to know that he had the support of Ittai and the six hundred men he led was encouragement indeed.

David had, also, the full support of the priests. Abiathar had proved himself loyal to the king over the years following the support David had earlier given him (*1 Sam 22:20–23*). Zadok was trusted by David who had made him joint high priest with Abiathar (*8:17*). David had no anxiety about the ark of God. He knew that Absalom was too shrewd to damage it; so the ark, the symbol of the divine presence, was taken back to Jerusalem, but David knew that God was with him. Had God withdrawn from him, these good, thoughtful people would not have stayed with him.

TO PONDER

When trouble comes, the seeds of goodness sown
  In happier days begin to bear their fruit;
Our God ensures that we are not alone,
  Of loyalty and friendship destitute.
And through his Spirit we become aware
  That we remain within his love and care.

Counter-Revolutionary Measures

2 Samuel 15:25–37

'The king also said to Zadok the priest, "Aren't you a seer? Go back to the city in peace, with your son Ahimaaz, and Jonathan son of Abiathar. You and Abiathar take your two sons with you" ' (v. 27, NIV).

Although David did not hesitate to evacuate Jerusalem, it is obvious that he was not prepared to give up the struggle which his favoured son had initiated. David knew he was at the disposal of God (*vv. 25b,26*) but until God made it clear that his reign was over, he would continue to fight.

Having left only ten concubines in the city, David knew that he needed a presence there that would give him information concerning Absalom's movements and plans. For this reason, he asked his two trusted priests to return, taking with them their sons who would act as messengers. The defection of Ahithophel to Absalom was a great blow to David (*vv. 12,31*). He knew the quality of Ahithophel's counsel and feared it. With great wisdom, therefore, he asked Hushai, who also counselled him, to return to the city and make Absalom believe that the king's two counsellors were at his service. Hushai, however, was commissioned by David to counter the advice given by Ahithophel (*vv. 32–37*). It was a shrewd and totally effective strategy.

The evacuation of the city was achieved with little time to spare. From the top of the Mount of Olives to the Temple area is only a short distance. Allowing for the slow movement of the elderly Hushai as he made his way to the city, the escaping king and his company must have been but an hour or so ahead of Absalom. As the record says: 'David's friend Hushai arrived at Jerusalem as Absalom was entering the city' (*v. 37*). If Absalom had been a better soldier he would have chased after David to destroy him before he could make good his escape and organise his defence. But God was not with Absalom.

TO PONDER   *Our Father-God has this intriguing way*
                         Of taking human choices, freely made,
                   And setting his creative grace to play
                         Around them, giving them his heavenly aid,
                   Until those bad decisions in the end
                   Reveal his power, our folly to transcend.

Hard to Bear

2 Samuel 15:23–37

'David continued up the Mount of Olives, weeping as he went . . . All the people with him . . . were weeping' (v. 30, NIV).

Our television screens have accustomed us to seeing large numbers of people who, caught up in war, are fleeing as refugees from their homes. The sight produces feelings of extreme sadness and sympathy, as we witness the tragedy unfolding before us. Although David's soldiers would give an air of order and strength to the long procession (if the record is true that the city, with the exception of ten concubines, was evacuated) the elderly and infirm, small children and babies were all on the march. Understandably, the people wept.

David would feel that he had been betrayed both as king and father. Absalom, a son he loved deeply, had deceived him and had proved true the rumours concerning his son's activities which David must have heard and had totally discounted. We can only imagine the depth of sorrow he felt. To weep was natural.

We are told that, 'The whole countryside wept aloud as the people passed by' (*v. 23a*). Not everyone was against David. Many remembered the situation under King Saul and knew how David had delivered them from those unstable days, and had built a kingdom of prestige and stability. They, too, had cause for tears.

Perhaps as he left Jerusalem David thought of his original conquest of the city, and the joy of the people as he established it as the capital city. He would think, too, of the circumstances which led to him being crowned as king – of Judah first and then of all Israel. David knew that Nathan's prophecy was coming true: 'Out of your own household I am going to bring calamity upon you' (*12:11a*); but he was obviously fearful that God had withdrawn support from him completely.

TO PONDER

How painful is the thought
Of God's withdrawn support!
How comforting to know
That God will with us go!
His presence makes the difference
Between despair and confidence.

Unwelcome News

2 Samuel 15:30–37

'Now David had been told, "Ahithophel is among the conspirators with Absalom" ' (v. 31a, NIV).

The historian gives no indication why Ahithophel chose to throw in his lot with Absalom. Ahithophel had already reached the pinnacle of his career with David, who valued his counsel greatly (*16:23*), and his new role with Absalom could hardly have been more prestigious than his role with David. Quite apart from his high status at David's court, Ahithophel was probably the grandfather of Bathsheba (*cf. 11:3; 23:34*). Although he may have resented David's liaison with Bathsheba, he would not have resisted her membership of the royal family. A further strengthening of Ahithophel's link with David should have been the fact that his son, Eliam, was one of David's mighty men (*23:34b*) – that courageous group dedicated to the service of the king. Even so, Ahithophel chose to defect to Absalom.

The loss of Ahithophel to Absalom was a serious personal blow. Absalom valued Ahithophel as highly as did his father, and David knew that the shrewd counsel given to Absalom would be followed; for this reason, David prayed, 'O LORD turn Ahithophel's counsel into foolishness' (*v. 31b*). The prayer had hardly been uttered when it seemed as though God had provided an answer. Hushai, bearing all the appropriate signs of a mourner, came to meet him on the Mount of Olives, and David probably felt that his presence was part of God's care of him (*v. 32*). As we have noted, Hushai became part of David's counter-measures (*WoL 5 Oct*).

In this instance, good counsel became foolishness when Absalom felt constrained to seek a second opinion, and Hushai, with a semblance of reasonableness and a measure of flattery, counselled Absalom to defer any immediate action (*17:1–14*). It was then that Ahithophel knew his betrayal of David had failed.

TO PONDER

God has preventive grace
  Which stops us doing certain things:
He has enabling grace
  From which our noblest action springs.
We each within our lives can trace
That God's way is the way of grace.

Opportunism

2 Samuel 16:1–4

'When David had gone a short distance beyond the summit, there was Ziba, the steward of Mephibosheth, waiting to meet him. He had a string of donkeys saddled and loaded with two hundred loaves of bread, a hundred cakes of raisins, a hundred cakes of figs and a skin of wine' (v. 1, NIV).

The disconsolate refugees from Jerusalem, having been made even more unhappy as they looked down on the city from the top of the Mount of Olives, must have been encouraged to see Ziba, his donkeys laden with provisions, standing at the roadside. They knew they were facing a long, hot descent to the Jordan valley and any refreshment would be welcome. Ziba's gesture meant that he had confidence in the victory of David over Absalom. Had he thought that David might not win the battle that must surely come, Ziba would have kept a discreet distance.

Of interest is the fact that David had only questions to ask. 'Why have you brought these?' and, 'Where is your Master's grandson?' (vv. 2,3). Ziba, it will be recalled, was the servant of Saul of whom David had earlier asked if there was anyone of the late king's household to whom he could show favour. It was Ziba who revealed that Jonathan had a crippled son by the name of Mephibosheth; David, therefore, took Mephibosheth, Saul's grandson, into his own household (9:1ff). The king could not understand why Ziba, on this distressing occasion, was not accompanied by Mephibosheth, hence the question. Displeased with what Ziba told him, David took back the lands he had given Mephibosheth (9:7) and gave them to Ziba (v. 4).

Sadly, Ziba was not telling the truth (19:26–29). It was for reasons of personal gain that he chose to be an opportunist. He would have served David, Mephibosheth and himself much better by displaying integrity. Truth is always better than falsehood.

TO PONDER   *The truth is always stronger than a lie,*
    And truthfulness a better crop will show;
For truth, which is of God, will never die,
    In fact, its influence will ever grow.
Truth builds up people, strengthens them and heals;
It is the currency in which God deals.

Permanence and Security

Luke 14:16–24 (following Sunday 3.10.99)

'The first said, "I have just bought a field, and I must go and see it.
Please excuse me" ' (v. 18, NIV).

A gracious host – in this case a gracious God – invited people to his
banquet and for varying reasons they rejected his invitation. He offered
them everything a hospitable, all-powerful, all-loving God could offer,
but they had other interests and chose accordingly. As he developed his
parable, our Lord referred to the guest who had just bought a piece of
land and who 'must go and see it' (*v. 18*). Unlike many other possessions,
land cannot be picked up, removed and hidden by thieves – the land
would be there still the next day – but the proud new owner 'must'
['must needs' (*AV*)] 'go and see it'.

The possession of land represents permanence and security. This new
owner, his family and generations as yet unborn, now owned a portion
of this amazing world which had whirled through the heavens and
sustained life since its creation, and which will continue to do so until
the end of time. The mysteries of seed-time and harvest were to be
displayed on *his* field. We understand the owner's delight but if, as we
suspect, he felt it gave him a touch of permanence and security, he was
wrong. As we may all discover sooner or later (*12:16–21; WoL 4.11,
July 99*).

Permanence and security belong not to this material world, but to the
spiritual world of which God – the host in our parable – is the supreme
ruler. It seems remarkable to us that this man had just told God that he
would rather look at his field than share in the feast of the eternal
kingdom. Even so, one way or another, people have been doing this in
every generation. God is not on their list of preferences.

TO PONDER
>Security is not this world's to give,
>>Our life on earth is brief, impermanent:
>God plans for us a better place to live,
>>According to Christ's better covenant.
>And in our heavenly home we can be sure
>That we will be forevermore secure.

PRAYER SUBJECT   *Christian aid workers in other lands.*

Another Form of Opportunism

2 Samuel 16:5–14

'As King David approached Bahurim, a man from the same clan as Saul's family came out from there. His name was Shimei son of Gera, and he cursed as he came out' (v. 5, NIV).

If Ziba played the part of the opportunist because he thought the victory would still go to David, the victor of so many battles in the past, Shimei played the part because he thought David would lose. By any reading of history, Shimei was unjust in his accusations (v. 8). The record is clear. David could have slain Saul on more than one occasion: it was his regard for the one whom God had anointed that stayed his hand and caused him to stay the hands of others (cf. 1 Sam 26:2–11). Further to that, the account states clearly that the man who claimed to have killed Saul was killed at David's command for doing so (1:2–16). David honoured Saul with a great lament (1:19–27) and honoured the family by taking Mephibosheth into the palace, giving him a place at his own table just like one of his own sons (9:11).

Resentment had unbalanced Shimei's judgment but not until now had he felt it safe to express his hatred of the king. Abishai, the same man who had wanted to kill Saul earlier (1 Sam 26:8), asked permission to kill Shemai for his impertinence (v. 9). David, however, had not lost his kingly ways and said, with wise forbearance, 'My son, who is of my own flesh, is trying to take my life. How much more, then, this Benjaminite!' (v. 11). He was prepared to take the criticism as from God.

There is always wisdom in listening to those who oppose us. If there is truth in what they say, we can learn and amend our ways. On the other hand, if there is no truth in the charges, our gracious endurance is acceptable to God. 'Blessed are you when people insult you . . . and falsely say all kinds of evil against you' said Jesus (Matt 5:11; cf. 1 Pet 2:20;3:17).

TO PONDER

> *The critic's voice is one we all should hear,*
>   *Although his words within our hearts may burn:*
> *We need to see what others see so clear,*
>   *Because from critics we have much to learn.*
> *But if those words are false – born of a grudge,*
> *Our sure defence remains – God is our judge.*

A Brave Opportunist

2 Samuel 16:15–23

'Then Hushai the Arkite, David's friend, went to Absalom and said to him, "Long live the king! Long live the king!" ' (v. 16, NIV).

The designation 'David's friend' meant more than just a friendly relationship: it was the designation of a high status position within the king's court. Elsewhere, just as Ahithophel is described as the king's counsellor, so Hushai is described as the king's friend (1 Chron 27:33). At this crucial time for David, Hushai was to prove worthy of the title of friend on both personal and official grounds. Because David thought Hushai might be a burden to him if he joined the fleeing Israelites, we make the assumption that Hushai was elderly (v. 33). If, however, David had reservations about Hushai's endurance, he had no doubts about his initiative and bravery. To return to Jerusalem and become a counter-agent for David was a difficult and dangerous assignment but without hesitation Hushai accepted it (15:32–37). Discovery would mean instant death, but success would almost guarantee David his victory.

We note that when Hushai approached Absalom, Ahithophel, a dishonourable opportunist, was already there (v. 15). Absalom was suspicious of Hushai at first but, possibly influenced by the fact that Ahithophel, a long-established counsellor, had betrayed David, accepted Hushai as another new ally (vv. 17–19).

The quality of Ahithophel's counsel was apparent immediately. Whoever went in to a king's concubines had, by so doing, staked his claim to the kingdom (cf. 3:6–11). By doing as Ahithophel proposed, Absalom would be telling the people of the unbridgeable gulf that existed between his father and himself (vv. 21, 22). To take over the harem or its equivalent was an unforgivable insult for one king to give to another. Sadly, Absalom was prepared to make the breach with his father clear to all.

PRAISE   *God did not leave himself without a voice*
       Within the council-room of Absalom.
    Though David's son with freedom made his choice,
       God still had plans for his Jerusalem.
    Through Hushai he would voice a strategy
       Which held this city to its destiny.

A Frustrated Opportunist

2 Samuel 17:1–14

'Ahithophel said to Absalom, "I would choose twelve thousand men
and set out tonight in pursuit of David" ' (v. 1, NIV).

We have already noted the mystery behind Ahithophel's defection to the
cause of Absalom (*WoL 8 Oct 99*). The historian gives no grounds why
he should become disillusioned with David who had set such a high
value on his counsel (*16:23*). There is, however, no denying the good
sense behind his advice to Absalom that David should be attacked
without delay, because every moment lost added to David's chances of
success. In Ahithophel's counsel he emphasised that Absalom's men
should make it clear that they were seeking David only, and the people
could return to Jerusalem to take up their lives again as though nothing
had happened, apart from a change of king (*vv. 2–4*). God's response to
this was to make Absalom seek a second opinion (*v. 5*).

Having inspired Absalom to call in Hushai, God inspired Hushai with
a counter-plan. Hushai was careful not to discount the wisdom of
Ahithophel but insinuated doubt, with, 'The advice Ahithophel has given
is not good *this time*' (*v. 7*). With growing confidence, Hushai outlined
another strategy: he played on Absalom's fears (*vv. 8–10*), and pandered
to his vanity (*v. 11b*). Absalom, seeing himself as a conqueror (*vv. 11–
13*), settled for the new plan, as did all his leaders. Ahithophel's advice
would have given them victory, Hushai's counsel of wait, reinforce and
then attack, virtually guaranteed Absalom's defeat.

Ahithophel knew he would be killed when David returned in triumph;
he made his way home, therefore, to Giloh, put his affairs in order, and
then killed himself (*v. 23*). As the record says, 'the LORD had determined
to frustrate the good advice of Ahithophel in order to bring disaster on
Absalom' (*v. 14*). God had kept his word, although he did not will
Ahithophel's suicide.

TO PONDER *God has his own inimitable way*
Of making sure that his plans do not fail,
He can frustrate the thoughtful words men say
By making sure a different view prevails.
The Lord our God does not desert a plan
Because of pressure from a wilful man.

Intrigue

2 Samuel 17:15–23

'Hushai told Zadok and Abiathar, the priests, "Ahithophel has advised Absalom and the elders of Israel to do such and such, but I have advised them to do so and so" ' (v. 15, NIV).

When Hushai realised that his counsel to Absalom had been accepted and Ahithophel's counsel had been rejected, he lost no time in setting his communication system in motion. David would be tempted to camp this side of the Jordan because of the weariness of his people, but that could be dangerous. Hushai, therefore, wanted a message to be sent to the king, telling him that he must put the river between himself and any pursuing Israelite troops. Zadok and Abiathar entrusted a servant-girl with the task of taking the message to Jonathan and Ahimaaz, the two chosen runners who were staying at En Rogel (*v. 17*).

Unfortunately, Jonathan and Ahimaaz were observed and had to hide but because David was not without support in the region, the two runners were given shelter in a well. The top of the well was concealed and when Absalom's men arrived, they found no one. The false information they were given (*vv. 18–20*) allowed Jonathan and Ahimaaz to start their journey and if the road to link up with the king was long, it had the virtue of being downhill. When Hushai's message was shared with David he took immediate action. He and his people must have felt much more confident because of Hushai's faithfulness and the fact that the river Jordan was between them and Absalom (*vv. 21,22*).

What a painful, ever-expanding disaster rebellion is! Absalom's ambition had already proved to be very costly. It had divided people. Ahithophel, once a trusted counsellor, was on his way home to die. Absalom and thousands of his men were soon to die. And David's army would suffer much. Why God continues to love us is a mystery, but it comforts us wonderfully.

PRAISE

> We are unlovable, but not to God!
>   For reasons he best knows and understands
> He seeks to rescue and deliver us;
>   To hold us safely in his powerful hands.
> Regardless of our foolish, wilful ways,
> His boundless love for ever with us stays.

Advantages

2 Samuel 17:24–29

'David went to Mahanaim, and Absalom crossed the Jordan with all the men of Israel' (v. 24, NIV).

Events were to prove that Ahithophel's counsel was wise (*vv. 1–4*) and that God was wise to turn that counsel into foolishness (*15:31; 17:14*). If, because of the thoroughness of Absalom's preparation for rebellion, the advantage had been with him, his delay in taking military action began to place the advantages in David's hands. We remind ourselves, also, that God, the absolute and unassailable advantage, was on David's side.

Although Amasa, whom Absalom appointed as his military commander, was related to Joab, he was no match for him and the two other army commanders David was able to appoint (*v. 25; 18:2*). Further to this, David, as the defending leader, was able to chose the place of battle and as we shall see his military skills had not diminished with the passage of time.

An evidence of David's strategic skills is shown in the way he based himself on the city of Mahanaim (*v. 24*). He had city walls now between himself and Absalom's army. This was the city where Abner, to suit his own purposes, made Ish-bosheth king after Saul, Ish-bosheth's father, had died (*2:8–10*). When Ish-bosheth was murdered, David executed his killers and gave Ish-Bosheth a proper burial (*4:1–12*). The death of Ish-bosheth led the people he ruled to ask David to be their king (*5:1–3*), and this he became, without revenge and with much kindness. The people would know, too, of David's kindness to Mephibosheth (*9:10*).

Because of all this, David had considerable goodwill on his side. Three important people volunteered support for him (*vv. 27–29*), making it clear that David and his people, were welcome and would not lack provisions. Good leadership, wisdom and kindness in the past, were being amply repaid.

PRAISE

A kindly deed from years long past,
Like bread upon the waters cast,
Sometimes returns to bless today,
In a delightful kind of way.
In ways which are quite unforeseen,
God's love and mercy intervene.

The Decisive Battle

2 Samuel 18:1–8

> 'David mustered the men who were with him and appointed over them commanders of thousands and commanders of hundreds' (v. 1, NIV).

The impending battle seemed to roll the years back for David: his warrior-mind was as incisive and inspired as ever. Of the men he brought with him from Jerusalem, and those who joined him in Mahanaim, David formed three armies, each of which was led by a trusted and competent leader: Joab, Abishai, and Ittai (*v. 2*). David, and the thousands of men loyal to him, could have confidence in them. Even so, the armies of David were smaller than the armies of Absalom (*cf. vv. 7b,8*) but the advantages remained with David. He had gifted leaders and Absalom did not. At the insistence of his men, David stayed in the city, thereby depriving Absalom's men of a target, whereas Absalom became a liability to his men simply because he was a target. The death of David or Absalom would signal victory for the other side (*18:16*).

David chose the forest as a battlefield because this vastly reduced the value of a large army, and defence is usually easier to organise than offence, as this battle confirmed. The trees and undergrowth reduced the mass of Absalom's army to manageable groups, at the same time giving ample cover to David's men. Many of Absalom's men became disorientated in the forest and, losing their way, were lost to the conflict: 'More men disappeared in the forest than were killed' (*v. 8, LB, cf. NEB*). Ambitious and arrogant, Absalom had grossly under-estimated his father whose reputation as a warrior was made, in part, by his ability to lead small armies to victory against much larger forces.

If he had under-estimated his father, Absalom had disastrously under-estimated God. The brief history of kingship in Israel must have been known to him, and we wonder what made him think he could claim the crown without having been anointed by God.

TO PONDER

> *The one who disregards the will of God*
> *Has chosen to live very dangerously;*
> *Though God is slow to punish with his rod*
> *He excludes none who live unrighteously.*
> *But still, with patient love he seeks to win*
> *All those who choose to follow ways of sin.*

Independence and Prosperity

Luke 14:16–24 (following Sunday 10.10.99)

'Another said, "I have just bought five yoke of oxen, and I'm on my way to try them out. Please excuse me" ' (v. 19, NIV).

Progress is almost always exciting. When a farmer has worked hard and is able to purchase ten oxen, progress, excitement and pleasure are in the air. Although he would probably have seen the oxen at work before making a purchase, we can understand him wanting to see them yoked and at work in his field and functioning under his own, or an employee's, direction. What we cannot understand is why that pleasure could not be deferred for a few more hours. The oxen would have lost nothing in that short time and he, the farmer, could have shared in the feast and enjoyed his fresh acquisitions later.

Sociologists tell us that one of the problems with many people is that they have difficulty in deferring gratification. Whatever they *want* to do takes precedence over what they *ought* to do. Those who work with volunteers – and not only volunteers – can support that contention. In the parable, however, Jesus touched on a man's progress and we interpret the farmer's problems as being independence and prosperity. How we like to be independent of other people! How some people even like being independent of God! With a measure of bravado a man shrugs off responsibility towards his Maker, affirms that he is his own man, and gets on with his life. Sadly, prosperity fuels that kind of independence for some people. Experience tells us that it is our need that drives us towards God, and those who are rejoicing in their freedom and luxuriating in their affluence have no sense of need. If it is true that, in a spiritual sense, poverty has slain its thousands, prosperity has slain its tens of thousands. Not everyone handles prosperity well (*Matt 19:21–24*).

PRAYER

> *Keep my need, Lord, before me;*
> *Let me on your grace rely,*
> *And my faith, Lord, multiply,*
> *Be thou my prosperity.*
> *All that men would call my own*
> *I place gladly at thy throne.*

PRAYER SUBJECT   *Christians serving in isolated places.*

Another Forest Casualty

2 Samuel 18:9–18

'Now Absalom happened to meet David's men. He was riding his mule, and as the mule went under the thick branches of a large oak, Absalom's head got caught in the tree. He was left hanging in mid-air, while the mule he was riding kept on going' (v. 9, NIV).

It would be easy to say that the hair in which Absalom gloried (14:26) was the cause of his death, but it was much more than that. He was a vengeful man, consumed with ambition; manipulative, arrogant, proud and unloving. There is so little in the man's nature that engenders sympathy. Desperate to be king, he took all the wrong measures to achieve it. Had he chosen to be a good and godly man – that choice was open to him – the hand of God might have come upon him for a kingly role. But he only illustrated in his day the truth Jesus was to express later, 'all who draw the sword will die by the sword' (*Matt 26:52*).

David had commanded his army leaders, 'Be gentle with the young man Absalom for my sake' (*v. 5*). Perhaps because he knew his commanders would treat Absalom for what he was, a man guilty of treason, David was careful to give his command in front of the men. In one sense it was understandable – he was Absalom's father; in another sense, it was foolishness – because most people believed that the threat of Absalom would die only when he died. Joab, who slew Absalom as he hung by his hair, was to chide David about this in due course (*19:5–7*).

We applaud the courage and restraint of the soldier who reported to Joab that Absalom was trapped (*vv. 10–13*). We note also, that unless Absalom was unconscious as he hung, he must have been in great agony; but he did not plead for help or mercy. When he saw Joab approaching, Absalom must have known that he would be killed; it was a terrible end to a life that could have been lived so much more purposefully.

TO PONDER   *Each choice we make helps to decide*
The person we, in time, become;
If we but choose in God to hide,
To evil be both deaf and dumb,
Our every step the Lord will bless;
And crown our lives with righteousness.

Different Perspectives

2 Samuel 18:19–27

'Now Ahimaaz son of Zadok said, "Let me run and take the news to the king" ' (v. 19a, NIV).

In his youthful eagerness to bear good news to the king, Ahimaaz, a runner of some repute (*v. 27*), was anxious to carry the news from the battlefield to David, who was waiting in Mahanaim. Ahimaaz lacked the experience to know that although the news of Absalom's death was good news to David's men, it was not good news to David himself. Joab, as calculating as ever, knowing that there were no rewards for the messenger who carried bad news (*v. 22b*), ordered a Cushite to carry the message instead.

Ahimaaz persisted in asking Joab who, after the Cushite had started, allowed him to run. As expected, Ahimaaz ran faster than the Cushite and, on arrival, having made his first statement to the king, he knew then why Joab had insisted on the Cushite delivering the message. David's major concern was Absalom (*vv. 28–29*). The Cushite was more thoughtful than Ahimaaz, and when he arrived a few moments later he presented his 'good news' in the kindliest terms possible. Although David, as king, would be glad that his army had been victorious, as Absalom's father, he was devastated by the death of his son.

The story raises an interesting and important point regarding the delivery of bad news. Most people today would prefer to receive such news from a person they respected and trusted. The quality of the relationship, the tenderness and concern in the voice, the body language, the immediacy of support, the reaching out of one spirit to another in genuine sympathy – all combine to provide a helpful means of grace and, if a blow can be softened, it will be softened in this way. Not so, apparently, in those days. The good man brought good news (*v. 27b*) and a neutral person carried the bad.

TO PONDER

Not one of us would ever choose
To bring a message of bad news;
But when such news is in our care,
May we, with deep compassion share
That news, and share our confidence
In God's great love and providence.

The Father's Grief

2 Samuel 18:28–33

'The king asked, "Is the young man Absalom safe?" ' (v. 29a, cf.32a, NIV).

The grief of David touches the heart. We see and hear him asking, first Ahimaaz, and then the Cushite, the direct question: 'Is the young man Absalom safe?' Ahimaaz gave a vague answer (*v. 29*), but the Cushite, although not confirming Absalom as dead, couched his reply in such a way that David knew that as far as he was concerned the worst had happened (*v. 32*). A broken man, David ascended the steps in the tower to a room above uttering the heart-rending words, 'O my son Absalom! . . . If only I had died instead of you – O Absalom, my son, my son!' (*v. 33*).

Perhaps the grief of many parents has caused them to say much the same kind of thing. How they would have preferred to suffer themselves than have their child suffer! David's case, however, is quite different from any other. *His* son had rebelled against him; *his* son had approved a strategy which aimed at his death (*17:1–4, cf.18:3*); *his* son, ruthless and self-seeking, would have killed anyone who opposed him, and have ruined the kingdom and was, therefore, hardly worth mourning. This David's men well knew, but David still mourned – was still heart-broken.

David had received so much from God: he had been anointed, and later crowned as king, given victory over Goliath and the Philistines, protected against Saul, honoured as the king, granted unique spiritual insights, and still he committed the crime of arranging the murder of the man whose wife he had stolen. Nathan's prophecy was understandably severe: 'Out of your own household I am going to bring calamity upon you' (*12:11–12*). Somehow, from that mysterious confluence of David's sin, divine restoration, and Absalom's freedom, came the rebellion. Neither the prophecy nor the principle are for anyone else to take to heart, but it helps us understand David's grief a little more.

PRAYER

We trust you, Lord,
We trust ourselves within your care,
Your answer to each need-filled prayer.
We trust the plans you have for us
To make us strong – victorious.
We trust you, Lord, and love you, Lord.

A Timely Rebuke

2 Samuel 19:1–8a

> 'Joab was told, "The king is weeping and mourning for Absalom" '
> (v. 1, NIV).

Large numbers of men had been prepared to die for David as they defended him against his rebellious son. All had been subjected to the rigours of warfare, many had been wounded and some had died. But what should have been an occasion of rejoicing had been turned into an occasion of mourning (v. 2). The soldiers who had served David so well were nonplussed: it was almost as though their hard-won victory was against the king's will.

Joab, David's army leader, whose confidence appears to have grown through recent events, was concerned not only for the nation but for David also, and told him the home-truths he needed to hear. 'You love those who hate you and hate those who love you,' he said, adding, for good measure, 'I see that you would be pleased if Absalom were alive today and all of us were dead' (vv. 5,6). With his indignation running high, Joab went on to counsel his king, 'Now go out and encourage your men' (v. 7).

Very much to David's credit, he accepted the rebuke. He offered no defence for his behaviour, ignored his right to stand on his kingly authority and made his way back to the gateway, to the very place where he had heard the bad news of Absalom's death, and made it plain that he wanted to see his men. As the word spread that David was waiting for them, the men who had been prepared to give him everything massed around him (v. 8).

There is an art in receiving a rebuke and, it would appear, David had developed it (cf. 12:13a). Correction, rebuke or advice to some people seems to spell rejection, but not so David. Even though what he did was understandable, it was wrong, and he was man enough to admit it. His prompt, positive reaction would serve only to increase the loyalty of his men.

PRAYER
O Lord, I am not always wise,
And things which seem right in my eyes,
Odd must appear in my friends' view
And make them wonder what to do.
Help me, when errors I am made to face
To do so with good sense, and healing grace.

A Leaderless Nation

2 Samuel 19:8b–15

'Throughout the tribes of Israel, the people were all arguing with each other, saying, "The king delivered us from the hand of our enemies ... But now he has fled the country because of Absalom"' (v. 9, NIV).

Following the death of Absalom, David did not return in triumph to Jerusalem as the conqueror to reassert his rule; instead, he continued to live in Mahanaim because he wanted the people to ask him to return as king. It did not take long for the tribes to realise that they had been duped by Absalom and that David should be reinstated. As the arguments about the kingship were rehearsed, dominant in the public mind was the fact that David had been their deliverer; he alone had defeated the Philistines and, no doubt, some would add the names of other nations he had overthrown (v. 9). David would find comfort in this, but he was disturbed by the silence of Judah, his own tribe (vv. 11,12).

Zadok and Abiathar, who had served the king so well during the evacuation from Jerusalem, became key figures in David's proposed return. He asked them to approach the elders on his behalf. They were to point out that David was their own 'flesh and blood' and ask why, when the rest of Israel wanted him to return, they had made no overtures to him.

David made the surprising proposal that Amasa, whom Absalom had appointed as head of his army (17:25), and which had failed so badly (18:7), should replace Joab, thereby becoming commander of the victorious army (v. 13). This unforeseen move might have been linked with David's belief that Joab was becoming over-confident but more likely it was his way of saying that there would be no reprisals against the rebels. The ploy was effective because we read that, 'He won over the hearts of all the men of Judah as though they were one man', and they sent word to him, 'Return, you and all your men' (v. 14).

TO PONDER

> Revenge does not become
>   The anointed of the Lord;
> Such feelings we must shun
>   And help create accord.
> If we would serve a loving God,
> Love's road is that which must be trod.

A Sense of History

2 Samuel 19:14:15

'Then the king returned and went as far as the Jordan. Now the men of Judah had come to Gilgal to go out and meet the king and bring him across the Jordan' (v. 15, NIV).

For the best of reasons, David did not want to appear too anxious to resume his role as king. The rebellion had won a surprisingly large measure of support in the land and he wanted to rule by consent, not by the force of arms. After his decisive victory in the forest of Ephraim (*18:6–8*), he knew that he could afford to wait for the public's favour to gather momentum and flow towards him. He did not have to wait long.

We note with interest that David did not respond immediately. Rather, he left Mahanaim and made his way towards the Jordan there to await the arrival of the men of Judah. The men assembled in Gilgal, marched to the Jordan, crossed the river (*v. 15*) and recrossed it with David and his men (*vv. 39,40*). In all Israel, there was probably no location more suitable for David to be reinstated as king than Gilgal. It was the place which entered Hebrew history after the people of Israel had crossed the Jordan on dry ground at the direction of Joshua (*Josh 3:5–17*). They pitched their camp east of the river (*Josh 4:18–20*) and, in time, that site became the town of Gilgal. It was at Gilgal that Saul was confirmed as king (*1 Sam 11:14,15*), and it was there that he was guilty of the disobedience that marred his rule (*1 Sam 13:3–14*). It was at Gilgal also, where Saul committed the sin which, in the end, lost him his kingship (*1 Sam 15:12–35*).

David had worked it out very well, or rather God had worked it out well for him. In a situation so full of history and symbolic meaning, and surrounded by the men of Judah, David was reinstated as the king of Israel. If anything, the tragic events of recent days had tended to make his rule even more secure.

TO PONDER
　　　　　Some places have a special atmosphere,
　　　　　　　Where almost everything lifts up its voice,
　　　　　Proclaiming God himself is very near:
　　　　　　　A glorious fact in which we can rejoice.
　　　　　Such places lift and strengthen mind and soul
　　　　　By telling us that God is in control.

Significance and Responsibility

Luke 14:16–24 (following Sunday 17.10.99)

'Still another said, "I have just got married, so I can't come"'
(v. 20, NIV).

In any society marriage is of enormous importance and the newly-weds know that they have to forge a joint lifestyle that will fulfil them as individuals, and nurture them as a couple. A Jewish wedding was an event which usually attracted the entire village (*cf. Matt 25:1–11*), everyone conspiring to ensure that the marriage had a good start. So important was a marriage considered to be among Jews, that a newly-married man was exempt from warfare: he was granted one year to 'stay at home and bring happiness to the wife he has married' (*Deut 24:5*). Even so, marriage seemed to be a poor excuse to use in order to avoid accepting the generous host's invitation to a feast.

Marriage, of course, gives special significance to people. Although they do not lose their original peer groups, the marriage partners subordinate friendships and relationships to their need for togetherness. If that is not done then the marriage relationship could suffer in course of time. It is obvious, also, that with marriage comes other responsibilities: the setting up of a home, ensuring financial resources, relating well to the extended family and, in due course, making provision for a family. But since vows are taken in the presence and name of God, marriage should improve rather than diminish a relationship with him. To use marriage as an excuse to reject the invitation to this feast was as offensive as it was unrealistic.

Even so, there are those who use close relationships to justify damaging a relationship with God. Nevertheless, our heavenly Father expects us to give him precedence over everyone.

PRAYER   *If God, not man, has bound two hearts together,*
Do we not know the bonds will last for ever?
If God remains the centre of a marriage,
None can that marriage break, nor it disparage.
God's ways with us are always providential,
And love in marriage not coincidental.

PRAYER SUBJECT   *For more Christian homes.*

A Generous Victim

2 Samuel 19:15b–23

'Shimei son of Gera, the Benjaminite from Bahurim, hurried down with the men of Judah to meet King David' (v. 16, NIV).

Many people in Israel must have feared for their safety when they learned that Absalom was dead and David had retained his crown. Some people might have feared a blood-bath when they learned of Absalom's death. Treason has always been taken very seriously, and those who had deserted David for Absalom were guilty of that. Shimei was not guilty of treason in the same way as many others, but he had taken opportunity to abuse the king verbally, and throw stones at him and his entourage (16:5–13). Bereft of comfort following the collapse of the rebellion, he had some work to do in rebuilding bridges with his monarch.

When the men of Judah left Gilgal and crossed the Jordan to meet David, Shimei was careful to be numbered among them (*v. 16*). He was careful, also, to be one of the first to reach the king and began to pour out his protestations of guilt and regret (*vv. 19,20*). At some time or other, most of us have been guilty of saying and doing something foolish, but nothing compared with the foolishness of Shimei. His crime was so distasteful that Abishai, brother of Joab, wanted permission to kill Shimei on the grounds that 'He cursed the LORD's anointed' (*v. 21*). David, apparently weary of the killing habits of Joab's family, 'the sons Zeruiah' (*v. 22*), denied Abishai his wish.

In David's judgment, this was not a day for recriminations and revenge, but a day of rejoicing. He was in the process of having his kingship renewed: why should he spoil it by spilling more blood? Indeed, why should he not enhance the day by exercising the right to be generous? This was the option he chose – it was in keeping with the mood of the day, and it would help to set the pattern for the reunification of his people.

PRAISE

> *What marvellous power forgiveness holds!*
> *It closes wounds and opens hearts,*
> *Its spark the light of new hope starts,*
> *Its warmth the fearful soul enfolds.*
> *Forgiveness is to future good the key,*
> *And is best given with generosity.*

Another Generous Victim

2 Samuel 19:24–30

'Mephibosheth, Saul's grandson, also went down to meet the king. He had not taken care of his feet or trimmed his moustache or washed his clothes from the day the king left until the day he returned safely' (v. 24, NIV).

It will be recalled that Mephibosheth was the sole surviving son of Jonathan and to him David showed kindness, even granting him a place at his table as though he were a son (*9:1–13*). Ziba, when he met David and his people with provisions as they escaped from Jerusalem, informed David that Mephibosheth was remaining in Jerusalem 'because he thinks, "Today the house of Israel will give me back my grandfather's kingdom."' Annoyed by this, David told Ziba that the land he had given to Mephibosheth and Ziba to share, was now his alone (*16:1–4*).

The recorder makes it clear that Mephibosheth, far from being a traitor, had remained loyal to David. From the time David left the city, Mephibosheth had mourned for him, and his unkempt appearance was the proof. When David asked why Mephibosheth had not left with him as a family member should, Mephibosheth revealed the duplicity of Ziba. The ass on which Ziba had ridden to meet David on the way from Jerusalem, was the animal which should have carried Mephibosheth. Ziba had carried his disloyalty even farther by telling the king that Mephibosheth was hoping for the kingdom to be returned to him (*vv. 26–28; 16:3*). Perhaps David was a little uncertain whom he should believe. In consequence, he ordered that the original instruction regarding the sharing of Saul's land should stand (*v. 29; 9:7–11*).

Mephibosheth's indebtedness to David was such, and his pleasure at David's return so genuine, that he renounced immediately any claim to the land. It could belong to Ziba. Rather than tussle with Ziba and his family for the land, he, Mephibosheth, would rejoice in his master's restoration as king (*vv. 29,30*).

TO PONDER
> *When matters of contention rage,*
> *With hearts not easy to assuage,*
> *We can resort to generosity –*
> *Feel love's divine immensity –*
> *Then gladly yield our rights with open hand,*
> *And find that nearer to the Christ we stand.*

More Goodwill

2 Samuel 19:31–40

'Now Barzillai was a very old man, eighty years of age. He had provided for the king during his stay in Mahanaim, for he was a very wealthy man' (v. 32, NIV).

Not at any time had David been without friends. Indeed, it could be claimed that his open and generous personality had won him many friends throughout his entire lifetime. In his early days, when he was a fugitive from Saul's court, his fairness gained him much support and, it will be remembered, when he had the opportunity to avail himself of plunder, he chose to share it with a large circle of friends and acquaintances (*1 Sam 30:21–31*). We do not know how his friendship with Barzillai began, but its strength was shown in Barzillai's willingness to risk the wrath of the usurper Absalom by his friendship. Materially, too, the friendship was costly. Making provision for David and all his people must have been an expensive exercise (*v. 32*).

Despite his age, Barzillai accompanied David to the Jordan where the grateful king asked him to continue with him to Jerusalem and be his guest (*v. 33*). Barzillai pleading his age and infirmities and his need to be near to the family tomb, suggested that his son, Kimham, should receive the king's hospitality instead (*vv. 34–38 cf. REB, GNB*). To this, David agreed happily.

There is no account of the ceremony, if such there was, whereby David was reaffirmed as the king of the twelve tribes of Israel (*v. 40*). We do not know whether the event was dominated by military or religious leaders, or whether someone had organised a balanced ritual of acceptance and commitment, but whatever it was it must have been acceptable to all present and to the nation. As David returned to Jerusalem in triumph, his thoughts must have dwelt on the hurried, almost chaotic way in which they had begun their enforced, although brief, exile. But he had the assurance that God was still with him.

TO PONDER

We cannot be where God is not,
No place exists which God forgot.
Wherever we, his people are,
Be that place near or be it far,
With confidence we can our trials face,
Since God is present with enabling grace.

Dissension

2 Samuel 19:41–43

'Soon all the men of Israel were coming to the king and saying to him, "Why did our brothers, the men of Judah, steal the king away and bring him and his household across the Jordan?" ' (v. 41, NIV).

Real life has always been short of 'living happily ever after' stories. A period of peace is, more often than not, shattered by discord. If David thought that the issue of his kingship was finally settled, the troubles could be considered over, and he could concentrate on ruling and judging the people, those involved in the earlier problems were about to prove him wrong.

Slightly confusing is the use of the term, 'men of Israel' as opposed to the term, 'men of Judah'. 'Israel' frequently means all the people, that is, all the twelve tribes. However, after the death of Saul, the tribe of Judah was loyal to David (*2:1–4*), and the remaining tribes were loyal to Ish-Bosheth and they were known as 'Israel' also (*2:8–11*). To confuse us further, after the death of David's son Solomon the kingdom was formally divided; the northern kingdom was made up of ten tribes with Jeroboam as king of Israel, and the southern kingdom having the tribe of Judah and much of the tribe of Benjamin. Rehoboam, a son of Solomon, was crowned the king of Judah (*cf. 1 Kgs 12:21*).

Because the men of Israel felt that David was favouring his own tribe of Judah (*v. 41, cf. vv. 11–17*), and that the men of Judah were treating them with contempt, they began to complain. As they said, 'We have ten shares [the ten tribes] in the king', and they pointed out further that they, and not Judah, had been the first to 'speak of bringing back our king' (*v. 43*). If reconciliation was in David's heart, it was not in the hearts of the men of Judah. Foolishly, they responded to the legitimate complaints of the men of Israel by treating them even more harshly. How greatly they needed the wisdom of God!

PRAYER
Bestow on us, O Lord, your love of peace,
Grant the desire to make all warfare cease.
Come to our hearts, infill us with your calm,
Place in our hands your own wound-healing balm.
Let our poor world hear Christ say, 'Peace, be still',
And be convinced that peace is what you will.

An Ill-Sounding Trumpet

2 Samuel 20:1–13

'Now a troublemaker named Sheba ... sounded the trumpet and shouted, "We have no share in David ... every man to his tent, O Israel" ' (v. 1, NIV).

Our understanding of God makes us realise that the events recorded in these chapters are much more distasteful to him than they are to us, and we find them completely abhorrent. Again, we need to remind ourselves that these events took place a thousand years before Jesus came, through whom alone we know of the tenderness, love and righteousness of the Father, and we can hardly expect the Israelites to behave as though Jesus, in all his glory, had been revealed to them. Even so, these events are hard to understand. Without doubt, if the price of human freedom is high for humanity, it is high for God also.

Sheba, of Saul's tribe, Benjamin (*1 Sam 9:1,2*), and the same tribe as Shimei (*16:5*), possibly saw himself as the king of Israel, and sounded the trumpet and started another rebellion. David, unlike his son Absalom, knew that speed was of the essence if this rebellion was to be put down, and ordered his newly appointed commander Amasa (*19:13*) to assemble an army within three days and march after Sheba (*vv. 4,5*). Whether Amasa lacked drive or efficiency we do not know, but David's target was not met and David appointed Joab's brother, Abishai, as commander and sent him after the enemy (*v. 6*). Joab, affronted because Amasa had been preferred to him and further affronted by the choice of his own brother, was determined to rectify things, and this he did, with dreadful consequences (*vv. 8–10*).

This awful story tells us that God still lives in our world, and, in spite of everything, has hope, even for the worst of us. When we think of today's tyrants, with their twisted values and nauseating deeds, we can only be grateful for God's love, and the confidence he has in us to help him change our world.

PRAYER
We are your lights in this dark world aglow,
Help us to shine more brightly every day,
Help us your path of love and joy to show,
That more find Christ as light, and truth, and way.
And help us keep our eyes on your dear Son,
Through whom your brightest light on earth is shone.

A Wise Woman

2 Samuel 20:14–26

'While they were battering the wall to bring it down, a wise woman called from the city, "Listen! Listen! Tell Joab to come here so that I can speak to him" ' (vv. 15b,16, NIV).

Under the leadership of Joab (*v. 11*) David's armies pursued Sheba northwards through Israel. It appears as though the other Israelites who had responded to Sheba's challenge gradually dispersed until, arriving at the city of Abel Beth Maacah, the city which was to be the scene of their last stand, only clan members of Sheba were available (*v. 14, cf. GNB*). With the rebels inside the city and the massive gates barred, Joab had a siege ramp built against the city wall in order to break through (*v. 15*). For the population, the prospect of this king of warfare, which was not of their making, was horrifying.

The people of Abel Beth Maacah had a reputation for peace and wise counsel; war was not a way of life for them, and a wise resident took resolute action. Braving any danger involved she called for Joab, who spoke with her. Emphasising the cherished role of the town as a 'mother in Israel' she enquired of Joab why he wanted to destroy the 'LORD's inheritance' (*vv. 18,19*). Joab's disclaimer, and that he wanted one man only, the rebel Sheba, met with an immediate response, 'His head will be thrown to you from the wall' (*v. 21*). The city leaders clearly thought that the death of the man who had caused the trouble was a reasonable price to pay to stop the war. Sheba was killed, Joab sounded the trumpet and his men left for their homes (*v. 22*).

War is brutal, costly and largely irrational because justice does not always require the movement of great armies across the land. Wisdom can often prevail and prevent the shedding of innocent blood. The major nations of the world are learning that lesson but, sadly, many other nations need still to learn it.

PRAYER
> *Give wisdom, Lord, to those who lead,*
>   *May those in power just now believe,*
> *That peace is still a world-wide need,*
>   *And, through you, peace we can achieve.*
> *Destroy the lust for power, that vain desire*
> *And let us to your perfect peace aspire.*

The Heart has its Reasons

Luke 14:16–24 (following Sunday 24.10.99)

'He sent his servant to tell those who had been invited, "Come, for everything is now ready." But they all alike began to make excuses' (vv. 17,18a, NIV).

What was the real reason, we wonder, why the invited guests chose not to attend the banquet? We ask because their reasons were so weak. In attempting to answer this question we conclude that the guests had established their priorities and the would-be host was not on their lists. We could press that statement a little harder and assume that they were no longer in harmony with their host; we could press it even harder and concur with Jesus that, since they were out of harmony with him, even hated him, they hated the Father also (*John 15:23; WoL 3 Oct 99*).

As a general rule, we do not accept invitations that would embarrass or discomfort us. We would not normally sit at the table of a person, even of high status, if we disliked him, feared him or were hostile to him. The people, therefore, who snubbed the host in our Lord's parable did so because they simply did not want to be associated with him in any way. They would rather look at a field or their oxen (*vv. 18,19*) than be with him.

We who know God, having learned of him through Jesus (*John 14:9– 11*), recognise him as a God of infinite mercy and grace. His patience with us in spite of our wilfulness and repeated failures, amazes us. Our gratitude to him for his constant care, his plans for us and the resources he offers, and his way of revealing himself to us in prayer, all help to make us long to share fellowship with him. Our hearts have their reasons for loving him, and the hearts of those who resent and oppose him have their reasons also for refusing his gracious invitation.

PRAYER

> *My Maker and my King,*
> *To thee my all I owe;*
> *Thy constant goodness is the spring*
> *Whence all my blessings flow.*

(Anne Steele, SASB 616)

PRAYER SUBJECT   *For more Christian sportsmen and women to be role models for our young people.*

Paul – A Free Man

Romans 8:1–4 (following 13.05.99)

'Through Christ Jesus the law of the Spirit of life set me free from the law of sin and death' (v. 2, NIV).

As we continue to consider the kind of man Paul was, we recommence with this simple statement: he was a free man. But none knew better than he that he had not always been free. We glance back to the first account of his conversion (*Acts 9:1–19*) and note that any man who was breathing out murderous threats against other people, who had felt it necessary to arm himself with authority to make prisoners of Christians and take them back to Jerusalem in triumph (*Acts 9:1,2*), was in bondage to evil of the most dangerous kind. To do evil things in the name of God is to move perilously close to committing the unforgivable sin (*Matt 12:30–32*). So impaired was his judgment, and so fierce the flames of anger within him, that he was capable of almost anything. At that time, he was not a free man.

In his testimony to the Romans, Paul confessed that the ancient law, which was the pride of his nation, had become a form of bondage to him. As a man anxious to be faithful to God, he was aware of the eternal struggle between good and evil within his soul. He wanted to do what the law said he should, but was aware of the law's inability to help him achieve that goodness. What he should be, and what he was, tormented him (*7:14–24*). He longed for freedom and could not find it.

The graciousness of Christ in accosting Paul on the Damascus Road was to end his bondage. When Ananias went to the house of Judas on Straight Street to meet the blind apostle-to-be, and laid his hands on him saying, 'Brother Saul, the Lord . . . has sent me so that you may see again and be filled with the Holy Spirit' (*Acts 9:17*), Saul, becoming Paul, found the freedom for which he longed. Life, for him, was never to be the same again.

PRAISE
Praise to the Lord! his Spirit's breath
Gives freedom from the law of death.
His Spirit is of life the law
Which frees us from our inward war.
The sin that held us in its chains
Has gone, because Christ Jesus reigns.

Free – from Condemnation

Romans 8:1–4

'Therefore, there is now no condemnation for those who are in Christ Jesus' (v. 1, NIV).

Paul's account of his conversion is recorded three times in the Acts of the Apostles (9:1–19; 22:1–16; 26:9–18), and we can be sure that in his many travels he told the story often. We take note that, although he had sinned grievously against God and his people, and the knowledge of his wrongdoing was never far from his mind, he did not carry a burden of condemnation as a result. His sins were forgiven: as he said to the Corinthians, 'If anyone is in Christ, he is a new creation; the old has gone, the new has come!' (2 Cor 5:17). Paul was not proud of what he had done, but part of the effect of the past upon him was to make him declare with great conviction, 'Christ Jesus came into the world to save sinners – of whom I am the worst. But for that very reason I was shown mercy so that in me, the worst of sinners, Christ Jesus might display his unlimited patience as an example for those who would believe on him' (1 Tim 1:15b,16).

Forgiveness, and the life of the Spirit, meant that Paul was not carrying the unwanted baggage of his past around with him. He was no longer condemned – no longer guilty; he was free from all of that and free to become the kind of man God wanted him to be. Free, in fact, to be 'in Christ'. What a marvellous work of grace our Lord has done for all of us! His work of redemption on the cross is a complete, not a partial work.

For some Christians this news is too good to be true, and they are inhibited by things said or done in the past. In one sense, that is understandable, but it must be much more reasonable to assume that 'sin will not have dominion' over us (6:14 RSV).

PRAISE

No condemnation now I dread;
Jesus, and all in him, is mine,
Alive in him, my living head,
And clothed in righteousness divine,
Bold I approach the eternal throne
And claim the crown, through Christ, my own.

(Charles Wesley, SASB 283)

Free – from Fear

Acts 16:16–28

'Finally, Paul became so troubled that he turned round and said to the spirit, "In the name of Jesus Christ I command you to come out of her!" At that moment, the spirit left her' (v. 18b, NIV).

Of the many examples of Paul's fearlessness, this is the one we will consider. Paul and Silas had left Asia Minor because he had received a vision of a man begging him to 'Come over to Macedonia and help us' (*v. 9*). Believing this to be of God they boarded a boat and arrived in Neapolis (*v. 11*). By this landing, the gospel had reached Europe. From Neapolis they travelled to Philippi and their first recorded convert was 'Lydia, a dealer in purple cloth from the city of Thyatira' (*v. 14*). Paul and Silas were being harassed in the street by a girl whose owners made money from her fortune-telling. Unable to contain himself any longer, Paul turned to the girl and commanded the spirit of divination to leave her (*v. 18*). Paul must have known that the consequences of depriving these men of their livelihood would cause trouble but he was free from any fear of them.

What follows was probably predictable. Paul and Silas were dragged before the authorities, the crowd joined in and, with no support in this new city, they were flogged and put into an inner prison cell, their feet firmly fastened in the stocks (*vv. 19–24*). Instead of being subdued by their pain and imprisonment, Paul and Silas sang hymns and prayed. They appeared not to be unduly concerned when an earthquake shook the foundations of the prison, and were quick to take advantage of the confusion created by the earthquake, to help the gaoler (*vv. 25–28*).

Presumably, Paul's inner strength came from his acute awareness of the presence of the risen Christ. In a later conflict situation Paul reported that 'the Lord stood near . . . and said, "Take courage!" ' (*23:11*). And that, Jesus always seemed to do.

PRAYER
> *The risen Lord dispels my fear,*
> *Because he is for ever near.*
> *His presence means I need not fail,*
> *His power means I must prevail.*
> *He keeps my feelings in control*
> *And makes me strong in mind and soul.*

Free – from Self-Pity

Acts 16:19–28

'About midnight Paul and Silas were praying and singing hymns to God, and the other prisoners were listening to them' (v. 25, NIV).

Cheerfulness would be in short supply in the prison where Paul and Silas had been placed. Perhaps, because Paul had demonstrated the supernatural powers of the exorcist and was, therefore, a man to be feared, he and Silas were placed in the inner prison. In addition to the normal chains which secured them to the wall, their feet were placed in wooden stocks. Bruised and bleeding from the severe flogging to which they had been subjected, they had cause to 'nurse their wounds' and reflect ruefully on their plight, but they chose to do neither.

The sheer discomfort of an ancient gaol, with its foul atmosphere, threat of physical violence, and constant use of violent language is hard for us to imagine, but Paul and Silas accepted it with joy – the kind of joy Christians can find in a variety of trials (*cf. Rom 5:3; Jas 1:2; 1 Pet 1:6*). Instead of indulging in self-pity, these two unjustly ill-treated men indulged themselves in the grace which God has made available to his people for all situations (*cf. 2 Cor 12:9,10; Phil 4:10–13*). We do not covet suffering of any kind, but we can be confident that when it does come, God's grace will prove to be sufficient.

Paul's life was oriented around the Lord Christ. As a servant he knew that if his Master had to suffer, he would not be exempt from similar trials (*John 15:20*): this seems to have saved him from a corrosive absorption with his own problems and cares. Their incredible freedom from self-pity enabled them to express a true missionary spirit at all times because, wherever they were they were still witnesses. In the providence of God they were soon to prove that the gaol had become a missionary objective and souls were to be won for Christ's kingdom.

PRAYER

O Christ, who died with arms outstretched in love
For all who lift their faces to thy cross,
Fill, thou, our lives with charity divine,
Till thou and thine are all, and self is loss.

(*Catherine Bonnell Arnott, SASB 181*)

Free – from Rationalisations

Acts 16:25–34

'About midnight Paul and Silas were praying and singing hymns to God, and the other prisoners were listening to them' (v. 25, NIV).

Arising from their joy in salvation and the experience of the Risen Christ, and in spite of their extreme physical discomfort, these two men of God began to pray and sing. Had we been in their place we might well have felt that such activity was inappropriate. We might have begun to rationalise and persuade ourselves that we had already been punished enough and any kind of disruption might make our plight worse. We could have argued that in those primitive and dangerous conditions, where other prisoners could take justice into their own violent hands, discretion and good conduct were called for, hopefully to gain any advantages given to model prisoners. Perhaps, so we would reason, we might win an earlier release, which would allow us the freedom to continue with a positive witness.

The scriptural account seems to suggest that these rationalisations never even crossed the thresholds of their minds. Because that was so, they prayed and sang hymns and, remarkably, the other prisoners listened. Presumably, the atmosphere of the gaol had often been pierced by cries of pain, shouts of defiance and crudeness. Prisoners' prayers, if any were made, would be silent and not many prisoners would know the words of Christian hymns. But Paul and Silas prayed and sang. Their prayers were probably of thanksgiving and might well have contained petitions for their persecutors, other prisoners and the gaoler (*Matt 5:44*). Such prayers and hymns – the latter probably being psalms – would be worth hearing and helpful to the others.

To them, the good news was always worth sharing, and where better, what place more suitable for such sharing, than a prison? They felt free enough to share, and God blessed them.

PRAYER

Lord, save me from my limitations,
My feeble rationalisations.
Just where I am, help me to share
The news that you are everywhere,
And help me to be strong and bold,
That love's great message may be told.

Free – from Hesitation

Acts 16:25–34

'Paul shouted, "Don't harm yourself! We are all here!" ' (v. 28, NIV).

What a story this is! If only Luke, our historian (*1:1; Luke 1:1–4*), had given us more detail, how much more colourful this incident would have been! But he was more concerned to present the story in a condensed form than to satisfy our curiosity. We wonder, for instance, whether the prisoners and gaoler associated the earthquake and opening of the prison doors with the obvious power and other-worldliness of Paul and Silas. Was the God to whom they were praying and singing responding with his own demonstration of power? Paul could not have seen the gaoler draw his sword with the intention of committing suicide because it was dark (*v. 29a*), and we are left to assume that a divine insight was given to him. Had Paul hesitated to act immediately on this guidance, the gaoler would have died.

Having called for lights, the gaoler rushed in to Paul and Silas and fell trembling before them (*v. 29*). Whether they asked him to release them from their chains and the stocks, or whether this was the gaoler's next initiative, we do not know, but he freed them, probably took them to his own accommodation, then asked the question, 'Sirs, what must I do to be saved?' (*v. 30*). Again, we do not know whether he had learned about Paul's mission from the witness in the city, or whether he had learned from the prayers Paul and Silas had made (*v. 25*); but the question was direct and completely sincere.

Paul's answer was equally direct and sincere, 'Believe in the Lord Jesus, and you will be saved – you and your household' (*v. 31*). Paul had no hesitation in taking the issue of salvation to the entire family and spoke the saving word of Christ to all, and he had no hesitation in confirming their salvation by baptising them in the faith, there and then (*vv. 33,34*).

PRAYER   *The seeking soul need never be dismayed:*
       Christ's word of mercy never is delayed.
    Once we believe, salvation is assured,
       And of its sin, each guilty heart is cured.
    Our Lord's great power instantly achieves
    A state of grace, when once the heart believes.

The Host's Reaction

Luke 14:16–24 (following Sunday 31.10.99)

'The servant came back and reported this to his master. Then the owner of the house became angry' (v. 21a, NIV).

On the assumption that in the parable the host is none other than Almighty God, we ought not to be unduly surprised at the fact that he responded to his rejection with anger. God is not bland, untouched by our inadequate responses to him and casual about our rejections. A God who cares deeply cannot retreat to another part of his universe and leave mankind to its own devices. The prime message of the Old Testament has to do with God's struggles to make the Hebrews into a 'kingdom of priests and a holy nation' (*Exod 19:6*). Israel's backsliding behaviour was an abhorrence to God, but he never ceased to love them (*Jer 31:3*). Further proof of the persistence of God's love is found in the Incarnation of our Lord, his death and Resurrection.

When we make our approach to our Father-God, we become aware of his feelings, of the the things he values and the things he cannot tolerate. More than that, we can understand his anger at the self-indulgence of those who should know better and who, because of that self-indulgence, choose to deny themselves the provision he has made for them. Another reaction by the host to their rejection of him was to send his servant out to bring the poor and distressed into his house to share the feast with him.

We note that it was the refusal of the guests that denied them their places around the table. The onus was on them because of the deliberate choice they had made. Of interest is the fact that the people who were commanded to come to the feast were the very people Jesus had said that the host and his friends should invite to their feasts (*cf. v. 21b, with v. 13*).

PRAISE

I hide me in the feelings of my God,
Who loves me with an everlasting love,
Who walks with me along my pilgrim road,
And waits to feast me in his courts above.
All that I need awaits my earnest prayer,
All that I am is safe with in his care.

PRAYER SUBJECT *Christians at work in shanty towns.*

Free – from Servility

Acts 16:35–40

'The jailer told Paul, "The magistrates have ordered that you and Silas be released. Now you can leave. Go in peace." ' (v. 36, NIV).

The magistrates had obviously concluded that a good flogging, a night in the cells and an earthquake were punishment enough for Paul and Silas; in consequence, they sent a message to the gaoler telling him to release Paul and Silas (v. 35). If the magistrates imagined that Paul was impressed and intimidated by their authority and the improper use they had made of it, they were about to be surprised. As Roman officials, the magistrates had gone beyond their mandate by punishing two fellow Roman citizens without a trial. They had been so anxious to be seen to be taking action against them that they had failed to determine whether Paul and Silas were Roman citizens or not.

As a citizen, Paul was law-abiding and respectful (Rom 13:1–7), but he was not servile; he was humble without losing respect or manliness. A grave injustice had been done to him and Silas, and those responsible could not be allowed to dismiss them without knowing that even magistrates had to obey the law. There was another, perhaps more important, consideration to make: if the magistrates felt that Christians could be silenced by a flogging and a night in the cells, they would continue to follow that policy. Paul needed, therefore, to make a stand in the interests of all those who would follow him and Silas to Philippi. As the account indicates, Paul was willing to be difficult.

It must have been quite salutary for the judiciary to visit the prison 'to appease them' (v. 39) and, although it was insisted that Paul and Silas should leave the city, they did so undefeated and with heads high. Luke records that they went to Lydia's house where they met the other members of the fledgling church, encouraged them, and continued their mission (v. 40).

PRAYER
   A thoughtful, firm and clear line must be drawn
    Between the standards which we know are right –
    Those standards which are noble in God's sight,
   And conduct which of justice has been shorn.
   God looks to us to honour all his ways,
   And keep the light of righteousness ablaze.

Free – from Bitterness

2 Corinthians 10:1–6

'By the meekness and gentleness of Christ, I appeal to you – I, Paul, who am "timid" when face to face with you, but "bold" when away.' (v. 1, NIV)

Although Paul, accompanied by Silas, left Philippi at the request of the authorities, his wounds, the legacy of his flogging, still painful, he left without bitterness. At some stage in his life Paul had probably learned that there were some negative emotions he could not afford to possess, and one of those emotions is bitterness. Bitterness clouds the vision, prevents growth, weakens prayer, robs the heart of joy, peace and love. Paul could no more afford bitterness than we can.

Some time after his expulsion from Philippi, Paul had the privilege of establishing the church in Corinth (*Acts 18:1ff*); it was probably his biggest challenge thus far. In spite of the problems presented by a culture which was steeped in iniquity, a church was planted and flourished. Although it continued to grow, divisions developed (*1 Cor 1:10–17*), and there were those in the fellowship who chose to attack him (*1 Cor 9:3*). Paul was hurt (*2 Cor 2:1–4*), but continued without bitterness.

As Paul remonstrated with his opponents he did so in the Spirit of his Master, 'by the meekness and gentleness of Christ' (*v. 1a*). Meekness and gentleness in Christ were not weak attributes; rather, they were part of his overall strength. A person is weak who cannot keep at bay the spirit of bitterness; who constantly rehearses the words or events that offended him and who lives in an atmosphere of recriminations of such strength that the whole of life is coloured by it. A person is strong who, when given cause for bitterness, refuses to entertain it and, turning to the Holy Spirit for the healing of his wounds, lives thereafter in the meekness and gentleness of Christ. Of such a character was Paul, the apostle.

PRAYER

O Holy Spirit, come,
And heal my wounded soul.
Heal me of bitterness,
And take complete control.
Let me Christ's graciousness reveal,
His love my motive and my seal.

Free – from Acquisitiveness

2 Corinthians 12:14–18

'I will not be a burden to you, because what I want is not your possessions but you' (v. 14, NIV).

It is always assumed that Paul came from a well-to-do family, but it was usual at that time, even for those who had no need to work, to be given a trade in case work became a necessity. The apprenticeship Paul served was that of tent maker (*cf. Acts 18:3*). It proved to be more valuable than his parents could have imagined, because by it he maintained himself and occasionally his companions (*Acts 20:34*) as he preached the gospel.

For apostles and evangelists who moved around the churches, it was expected that they would be supported by the various congregations. That was a right Paul refused to accept. Instead, he and Barnabas were self-supporting (*1 Cor 9:3–6, 15–18*), and not at any time did Paul make his needs known to the people. As he said to the Thessalonians, 'We worked night and day in order not to be a burden to anyone while we preached the gospel of God to you' (*1 Thess 2:9; 2 Thess 3:7–10*). When we consider the enormous work load he carried related to the care of the Church, we are amazed at his determination and industry as he refused to be a burden to any congregation.

Because of his stand on this issue of self-support, he could face any section in the Church: the wealthy, the less wealthy or the very poor. They had nothing material that he coveted because he was completely non-acquisitive, but he was desperate to have them, 'What I want is not your possessions but you' (*v. 14b*). Even in that great desire there was no acquisitiveness because he wanted them for his Master. 'We proclaim him [Christ]' he wrote later, 'admonishing and teaching everyone with all wisdom, so that we may present everyone perfect in Christ' (*Col 1:28*). Paul wanted people only so that he could give them to his Lord.

PRAYER

> Deliver me, O Lord, from wanting things,
>   From all the vain desiring envy brings:
> That, with a sanctified and open mind,
>   I might full joy and satisfaction find
> In doing just as you would have me do,
> And proving my dependence is on you.

Free – from Formalism

Philippians 3:1–6

'As for legalistic righteousness, faultless' (v. 6b, NIV).

One of the traps into which the unsuspecting Christian can fall is that of formalism. Although we know we live by faith, we can become so used to our symbols and procedures that we afford them a greater value than they possess, and fall into the errors of formalism. As a problem it was not new to Paul as the Council of Jerusalem shows (*Acts 15:5–21*), and his letter to the Galatians confirms. He was amazed at the ease with which they had moved from faith to formalism: 'Are you so foolish? After beginning with the Spirit, are you now trying to attain your goal by human effort?' (*Gal 3:3*) Here, then, in his letter to the Philippians, the apostle repeats the warning (*vv. 3–6*).

Paul begins by making it clear that he does not mind repeating himself (*v. 1b*): it is a fact of experience that we need constant reminders of important things. William Temple was certainly correct when he said that the most powerful sermon is often the one which tells us what we already know. And Paul emphasised his argument by pointing out that by birth, upbringing and personal choice, he had accepted the culture of law and ritual as the means of salvation. His zeal was obvious, even leading him to persecute the Church (*Acts 9:1,2*) and, he added, 'as for legalistic righteousness [I was] faultless' (*v. 6*).

It was the sheer strength of those legalistic bonds which made Paul rejoice in his liberty when Christ set him free; a freedom he revelled in and advocated throughout his ministry. In writing to the Colossians he expanded on this theme, 'See to it that no-one takes you captive through hollow and deceptive philosophy, which depends on human tradition . . . rather than on Christ' (*Col 2:8*). As we live 'in Christ' we have total freedom from the restraints of tradition and legalistic righteousness.

PRAYER

> *The freedom which the Spirit gives*
> *Is that by which the Christian lives.*
> *We are from lesser things set free,*
> *To share Christ's perfect liberty.*
> *Released from all our bonds, we find*
> *The grace to live our lives as God designed.*

Free – from Wrong Emphases

Philippians 3:7–10

'I consider everything a loss compared to the surpassing greatness of knowing Christ Jesus my Lord, for whose sake I have lost all things. I consider them rubbish, that I may gain Christ' (v. 8, NIV).

Everything that Paul had cherished under the law and through his association with Judaism – those traditions and values of which he was so proud (*vv. 4–6*) – now counted for nothing. The new life he had in Christ with its attendant freedoms had become so reasonable and valuable that he was able to say, 'I consider everything a loss compared to the surpassing greatness of knowing Christ'; he even described his former values as rubbish. God had initiated Judaism as a preparation for the Incarnation of his Son but Judaism, as a body of belief, had been damaged by the unfortunate development of trivial laws and traditions, and these were part of the 'everything' the apostle now regarded as loss.

One of Paul's outstanding characteristics is the high quality of his mind. Sample his writings anywhere and the largeness of his vision shines through. His thoughts are big thoughts because he had the freedom to think as his Master thought. Not for him an unfruitful association with the trivia of life; in Christ, he faced God's purposes for mankind and as a result his words have stimulated and motivated believers ever since. Were we to reflect upon Paul's desire to 'gain Christ and be found in him', we would find ourselves engaged in a most fruitful spiritual exercise, and the succeeding thoughts would lift us to new heights of knowledge and experience (*vv. 8–11*).

Even so, Paul's apprehension of the great truths of our faith never stopped him from being a practical person. Part of his value to us is that his feet were always firmly on the ground. The great truths he learned were always relevant to everyday life and in consequence we are enormously indebted to him.

PRAYER
Grant me, O Lord, the power to think
Thoughts simple, vital and profound.
Nor let me from this yearning shrink,
But make my zeal for truth abound.
I, too, would seek to know you, Lord,
And with you be in full accord.

Free – from Complacency

Philippians 3:12–14

'Not that I have already obtained all this, or have already been made perfect, but I press on to take hold of that for which Christ took hold of me' (v. 12, NIV).

There is always new ground to be claimed in the Christian faith and always fresh peaks to climb. What we already have is wonderful, but God has planned that there should be more ahead of us, and that is marvellous. In a world where human progress has often been marked in most dramatic ways, there is nothing to match the progress God has in mind for those who love him.

Compared with the apostle Paul many of us would consider ourselves to be novices only. We struggle at times, we seem to take two paces forward and one pace backwards, but God, through his Holy Spirit, has never finished with us. Always, he is urging us to serve him better and more imaginatively if health and circumstance permit, to pray better, exercise faith more specifically and grow in grace more. Above all, he wants us to become more Christlike. As Jesus took hold of Paul on the Damascus Road in order to fulfil the great potential of his life and make him a partner in the gospel, so he takes hold of us. In honesty and humility we would consider ourselves lesser people than Paul but Christ values us no less, and strives no less to help us become what we are meant to be.

Paul's great achievements never persuaded him that he had become the finished article. Although he was completely aware of the power of the Christ in whom he had believed (*cf. 2 Tim 1:12; Eph 3:20*), he never lost an awareness of his vulnerability. He knew that even he, with all that he had received from Christ, was free to make those choices that could disqualify him from the ultimate prize (*1 Cor 9:27*). For him, the future held more than the past and, gloriously, it is so with us.

PRAYER

> Make this poor self grow less and less,
>   Be thou my life and aim;
> O make me daily, through thy grace,
>   More meet to bear thy name.

(*Johann Caspar Lavater,*
trs Elizabeth Lee Smith)

The Open Invitation

Luke 14:16–24 (following Sunday 7.11.99)

'And the master said to the slave, "Go out into the highways and along the hedges, and compel them to come in, that my house may be filled" ' (v. 23, NASB).

The long and honourable history of the Christian faith has been occasionally sullied by zealous people who have misunderstood the meaning of this command. There have been times, for instance, when people have been compelled quite literally to accept the faith. Such behaviour in the name of Christ is not acceptable. Had God wanted to force the nations of the world to love and serve him he could have done it without our help but, instead of physical power, manipulation or coercion, he chose the power of love. It is true that those who reject him will be denied entry to his kingdom but by their own free choice they will have denied themselves the blessings he has to offer.

We have no mandate to twist arms or inflict punishment of any kind in order to lead people to faith. Our appointed method is Christ's chosen method, and that is the power of love. His command is, 'Love your enemies and pray for those who persecute you, that you may be sons of your Father in heaven' (*Matt 5:44,45a*); 'God did not send his Son into the world to condemn the world, but to save the world through him' (*John 3:17*).

Saul of Tarsus believed that he could use force to stamp out Christianity, but when he became a Christian he followed the way of love, which was the way of his Master. Writing to Timothy, Paul said, 'Preach the Word; be prepared in season and out of season; correct, rebuke and encourage – with great patience and careful instruction' (*2 Tim 4:2*). The compulsion of love is far stronger than the compulsion of physical force. Such ever was Christ's way and his way must be ours.

TO PONDER

> *Toil on, faint not, keep watch, and pray;*
> *Be wise the sinning soul to win;*
> *Go forth into the world's highway,*
> *Compel the wanderer to come in.*

(Horatio Bonar, SASB 683)

PRAYER SUBJECT — *Personal evangelism.*

Free – from Negative Memories

Philippians 3:12–14

'But one thing I do: Forgetting what is behind and straining towards what is ahead, I press on towards the goal to win the prize for which God has called me' (vv. 13b,14a, NIV).

This brief passage of Scripture (*vv. 12–14*) is charged with energy. Paul sees the Christian life as a race; not as a race where there is only one prizewinner, because all who run in the Christian race are counted victorious (*cf. 1 Cor 9:24–27*), but a race which requires everything we have and are if we are to succeed. In a race, as in the Christian race, the runner has to press forward with mind concentrated on the immediate task, and no thought for what may have happened previously. On this subject, J. Hugh Michael quotes from Chrysostom, one of the early Christian Fathers who said, 'The runner does not count the laps that are passed, but those that remain.'

It was remarkable that Paul, sitting in his prison cell as he dictated this letter, could even think of the metaphor of the race, but we are are glad that he did so. Enforced inactivity does not remove us from the course – we remain participants.

There are certain memories that inhibit our progress in the spiritual life; they slow us down by distracting us and weakening our concentration. What is done and forgiven is worth forgetting! There is a future full of challenge and opportunity stretching ahead of us; a future that needs all the dedication we can give to it. There are successes also in the past which, although enjoyable at the time and enjoyable still in retrospect, ought not to be consuming our energies as we run our race. Obviously, we can savour past victories, draw strength and inspiration from them, but we cannot rest on them. Those victories were yesterday: today and tomorrow require our attention. We are to forget what is behind and press on towards the goal.

PRAYER

> O let my life, Lord, focused be,
>   My heart and mind fixed on my goal;
> If I would win then I must be
>   Relaxed, intent, and in control.
> Be sure, O Lord, to keep before my eyes
> The truth that Christ is my life's goal and prize.

Free – from Anxiety

Philippians 4:4–7

'Do not be anxious about anything' (v. 6a NIV).

Having previously confessed to anxiety over the fact that Epaphroditus had been very ill and that he was now well enough to return home (*2:25– 28*), Paul, in continuing his letter, counselled the Philippians not to be anxious about anything! If, however, Paul had known how carefully every word he wrote was to be examined in later years, he might have chosen a different word from *anxiety* to describe his concern over the health and well-being of Epaphroditus. Even so, we take his word regarding anxiety to heart because we are ourselves often anxious, sometimes to a degree that we feel intuitively is not quite right.

Paul's advice was not new and was well-founded. The Master had counselled the disciples against undue worry (*Luke 12:22–31*) and he himself was the prime example of a worry-free life. Although our Lord's days were full to overflowing with activity, teaching, healing, conflict, and priorities that were of the greatest significance for the whole of mankind, he carried each day with the poise of a man confident of his place in the Father's plan. The theme was highlighted also by Peter. When he wrote to the relatively new converts in Asia minor who were on the brink of 'all kinds of trials' (*1 Pet 1:6b*), he said, 'Cast all your anxiety on him because he cares for you' (*1 Pet 5:7*).

Our Lord, Peter and Paul carried heavy responsibilities and did so conscientiously and devotedly. Not for them the mental detachment some people try to achieve; but they were not anxious because they knew to whom they belonged and in whose hands they were. Come fair weather or foul, their constancy related to a heavenly Father on whom they could depend. Because Paul had become a man of prayer, he knew that he could take everything to God and trust him for the future (*v. 6b*).

TO PONDER

> *O what peace we often forfeit,*
> *O what needless pain we bear,*
> *All because we do not carry*
> *Everything to God in prayer!*

> (*Joseph Medlicott Scriven, SASB 645*)

Free – from Discontent

Philippians 4:10–13

'I have learned the secret of being content in any and every situation, whether well fed or hungry, whether living in plenty or in want' (v. 12b, NIV).

Few people have been called upon to suffer as much for the sake of the gospel as Paul (*Acts 9:16*). When he was writing to the Corinthians and felt it necessary to defend his apostleship he 'boasted' of many of the privations he had endured (*2 Cor 11:23–33*). He compiled the list to God's glory, not because he had complaints about the way the Lord, or his people, had handled him but, as he said to the Philippians, 'I have learned the secret of being content in any and every situation' (*v. 12b*).

It was not as though he was in a delightfully relaxing situation when he wrote this letter to the Philippians. Scholars debate whether he was in Rome, Ephesus or Caesarea but all agree that he was prison (*1:12–26; 2:17*). To be content in any gaol represents an achievement, but for an activist, with the care of the churches on his heart (*2 Cor 11:28*), restlessness rather contentment would be expected. But Paul's word, 'I have learned the secret of being content' must be true because, 'I can do everything through him who gives me strength' (*v. 13*).

The contentment which characterised Paul was related to the enormous resources made available to him by Christ. It was related also to his confidence that his life was firmly fixed in the providence of the Father. Nothing could happen to him which could take him outside the Father's care, and everything that happened, of good or apparent ill, would work together to his benefit (*Rom 8:28–39*). With a confidence like that, we can understand why the apostle Paul was free from discontent.

TO PONDER
> *Only thy restless heart keep still,*
> *And wait in cheerful hope, content*
> *To take whate'er his gracious will,*
> *His all-discerning love, hath sent;*
> *Nor doubt our inward wants are known*
> *To him who chose us for his own.*

> (*George Christian Neumark,*
> *trs Catherine Winkworth, SASB 738*)

Free – from Recriminations

Philippians 4:10;14–19

'I rejoice greatly in the Lord that at last you have renewed your concern for me. Indeed, you have been concerned, but you had no opportunity to show it' (v. 10, NIV).

How generously Paul dealt with his people! He had ample cause to feel as though he had been left without support at a particularly vulnerable time in his life, but still he treated them with great tenderness; they had 'been concerned but . . . lacked opportunity to show it'. His sacrifices for them, the privations he had endured to bring the gospel to them, ought to have given him expectations of genuine concern from them, but they seemed to remain silent, and he did not appear to be unduly hurt.

In actual fact, when evidences of their care began to flow towards him he expressed his gratitude with much grace (*v. 14*) adding that he had not been 'looking for a gift, but I am looking for what can be credited to your account' (*v. 17*). He was happy to receive, but happier still to know that they were being credited by the Lord for possessing a generous spirit (*cf. Matt 25:34–40*). Their kindness so delighted Paul that he told them he had 'received full payment' (*v. 18a*). If ever they considered themselves to be in his debt because of what he had done for them, they had repaid that debt in full. But Paul did not leave it there; he wanted them to know that the gifts they had made to him were 'a fragrant offering, an acceptable sacrifice, pleasing to God' (*v. 18b*). He could not say much more than that.

In his relationships with his people Paul was extremely honest. The way in which he corrected them in his letters (*cf. 1 Cor 5:1,2*) reveals just how plain-spoken he could be, but always there was love (*4:1; cf. 2 Cor 7:2–4*). And it was because he loved them so much that he constantly credited them with the best of motives, and did not indulge in recriminations.

PRAYER
How do thy mercies close me round!
For ever be thy name adored!
I blush in all things to abound;
The servant is above his Lord!

(*Charles Wesley*)

Free – from Self-Assertiveness (1)

Acts 16:6–10

'After Paul had seen the vision, we got ready at once to leave for Macedonia, concluding that God had called us to preach the gospel to them' (v. 10, NIV).

The incident recorded in our chosen Scripture relates to Paul's second missionary journey. He had intended that Barnabas should be his companion, but Barnabas wanted Mark to accompany them. Paul was unhappy about that because of Mark's earlier desertion (*13:13*) with the result that Barnabas took Mark and Paul took Silas (*15:36–41*). The reference to 'his companions' (*v. 6*) meant that Timothy was now a missioner with Paul and Silas (*vv. 1–3*). Soon, Luke – the writer of Acts (*cf. Luke 1:1–3; Acts 1:1*) – would join them in Troas (*note: 'they' and 'we', vv. 8,10*).

Paul seemed to have no set plan for evangelism on this mission tour other than that of strengthening the churches (*15:36,41*), but he seemed to have in mind extending the work in Asia. Such was his sensitivity to the Holy Spirit, however, that he allowed himself to be guided away from his general intention (*vv. 6–8*) and at Troas he received the guidance which galvanised him into immediate action: they were to go to Macedonia (*vv. 9,10*).

From this incident we confirm the fact that Paul was not his own man – he was the Lord's. He had no plan other than his Master's plan. If the Spirit closed a door, he did not try to open it (*v. 7*), and when the Spirit opened a door, he passed through it. From the moment he became a disciple this deference to divine guidance emerged as one of his dominant characteristics. As Saul of Tarsus, he hounded the followers of Jesus. All his initiatives seemed to be self-generated. If he was guided at all it was by anger and an irrational zeal for the traditions in which he had been nurtured, and nothing, or no one, was going to stop him. But after his encounter with Christ his self-assertiveness was replaced by a natural compliance to his Lord's will.

PRAYER

O that in me the mind of Christ
A fixed abiding-place may find,
That I may know the will of God,
And live in him for lost mankind.

(*Edward Henry Joy, SASB 451*)

Free – From Self-Assertiveness (2)

Philippians 2:1–8

'Let this mind be in you, which was also in Christ Jesus' (v. 5, AV).

We follow yesterday's thoughts on self-assertiveness and the closing prayer about the 'mind of Christ', with further comments on this great subject. Paul's lack of self-assertiveness was due to the indwelling of the Holy Spirit – the Spirit of Christ (*cf. Rom 8:9*) and his determination to allow the Spirit to dominate him. He had yielded all rights to himself and had accepted the divinely-appointed right to strive after Christlikeness.

More today, perhaps, than ever before, people are concerned about individuality and the assertion and maintenance of personal identity. 'I am my own person.' 'That is how I see it and how I want it', 'You must respect my personhood', are among the statements used to indicate that personal choice, feelings and expression are all-important. A song which reiterated the line, 'I did it my way', probably owed its success to the fact that it resonated so well with the views of vast numbers of people. '*My way*' takes precedence over your way even, in the opinion and lifestyle of many, over God's way. Although it may sound reasonable, the entire sentiment is foolish and unrealistic. We have more than enough evidence, personal and otherwise, to prove that those who hold the reins of life in their own hands do not do well. Paul seemed to be thinking this way when he wrote to the Galatians, 'If anyone thinks he is something when he is nothing, he deceives himself' (*Gal 6:3 NIV*).

Except we have the mind of Christ we will have the wrong goals, values, attitudes, abilities and resources. Paul knew that, hence his advice to the Philippians (*vv. 5–11*). Because he had surrendered himself, Paul was able to add, 'I can do everything through him who gives me strength' (*4:13 NIV*). We do not merit it, but God has made available to us the mind of Christ.

PRAYER

O Christ, who shares all human life,
*   Let your mind dwell in me.*
Replace with love my inward strife,
*   And let me loving be.*
'My way' has done so little for my soul,
Come now to me, indwell me, make me whole.

Today's Feast

Luke 14:16–24; John 6:35 (following Sunday 14.11.99)

'Then Jesus declared, "I am the bread of life. He who comes to me will never go hungry, and he who believes in me will never be thirsty" ' (John 6:35, NIV).

As on every previous Sunday, countless millions of people will gather today in countless churches to worship God. Most have been redeemed by the sacrifice of Jesus; some have lost their faith but still attend for reasons which they may not even know; others are seeking a faith; others are present for social or family reasons. Since, however, Christ is present and as our key verse affirms is able to give sustenance to all who respond to him, there is a sense in which the gospel feast has begun.

Millions of people today will return to their homes from their churches and will feel nourished. After the Scriptures have been opened to them, some people will say, 'We have been well-fed from the word yet again', because the word of God has this remarkable way of strengthening and encouraging us. As Jesus said when his adversary tried to tempt him, 'Man does not live on bread alone, but on every word that comes from the mouth of God' (*Matt 4:4*). On the other hand, there might be other members of the congregation who, although blessed by the Scriptures, feel that by being part of a worshipping community, sharing fellowship in prayer and sharing experiences of Christian warfare have been particularly reinforcing activities.

Most people, however, will be aware that in a mystical, although a very real, sense they have been feeding on Christ who, having promised to be with his people, has fulfilled the promise. He is the bread and water of eternal life and he gives generously to those who believe in him (*John 6:35*). Surely, there can be no richer fare than that!

PRAISE

> He will feast me still with his presence dear,
> And the love he so freely hath given;
> While his promise tells, as I serve him here,
> Of the banquet of glory in Heaven.

> (*Sylvanus Dryden Phelps, SASB 373*)

PRAYER SUBJECT   *World evangelism.*

Free — from Pride

Romans 3:21–28

'What room then is left for human pride? It is excluded. And on what principle? The keeping of the law would not exclude it, but faith does' (Rom 3:27, REB).

In his letter to the Romans, Paul wrestles with some of the great themes of the Christian faith, and does so with enormous power and grace. Not for nothing is this letter so highly regarded, and counted as one of the most influential he ever wrote. To clear the way for his exposition of the doctrine of justification by faith (5:1ff.) Paul began by concluding that the whole of mankind had sinned and come short of the glory of God (v. 23 AV). Paul showed that the wrath of God is on the Gentiles because of their sin against the light they had already received (1:18ff.) and, just in case the Jews were preening themselves because of their 'righteousness', Paul revealed their faults to them, and punctured their complacency (2:1–3:20). As our key verse implies, if the Law could be properly fulfilled there would be cause for pride, but since that is impossible faith is required, and faith leaves no room for pride. We are saved by grace through faith, 'it is the gift of God – not by works so that no one can boast' (Eph 2:8,9 NIV).

On a purely human level Paul had much about which he could boast: his achievements were great and not many people could match his gifts. He did not boast, however, because he knew his own heart too well and knew, also, that whatever he possessed was a gift, and whatever he had done was by the enabling power of the Spirit. The only personal boast he allowed himself was in his weaknesses! To the Corinthians he wrote, 'I will boast about my weaknesses, so that Christ's power may rest on me. That is why, for Christ's sake, I delight in weaknesses, in insults, in hardships, in persecution, in difficulties. For when I am weak, then I am strong' (2 Cor 12:9b,10). If 'pride goes before a fall', dependence upon Christ is the guarantee of victory.

PRAYER

> All that once I thought most worthy,
>   All of which I once did boast,
> In thy light seems poor and passing,
>   'Tis thyself I covet most.

(Ruth Tracy, SASB 435)

Free – from Personal Ambition (1)

Colossians 1:24–29

'We train everyone . . . in order to set everyone before God mature in Christ; I labour for that end, striving for it with the divine energy which is a power within me. Striving? Yes . . .' (*vv. 1; 28–2:1, JM*).

We can only imagine how ambitious the young Saul of Tarsus was. The impression we receive is of a man who could not do things by halves and who always sought to excel. Possibly, this was the reason why his parents sent him to Jerusalem to study under the renowned Gamaliel. In all probability, this was the reason also why he was a leading figure in the persecution of Christians (*Acts 22:3–5*). We do not know what his ambitions within Judaism were but even as a young man he had made his mark.

It is clear, however, that the spirit of ambition as such died within him when he received the Holy Spirit, and he accepted an entirely new set of priorities. Although he made his mark as a witness in Damascus and Jerusalem he was compliant when it was felt that he should leave Jerusalem and return to his own city of Tarsus (*Acts 9:19b–30*). He remained there for a period sometimes called the 'hidden years', leaving only when Barnabas came for him (*Acts 11:25*). Ambition, in the usual sense, was no longer a part of him; through the Holy Spirit his goals had been changed. He had become Christ-centred. Nothing else mattered.

One of Paul's prime ambitions was to present to God people who had become mature in Christ. For this reason he proclaimed Christ and, since proclamation is not enough, he trained people in the knowledge of Christ (v. 28). It was an all-consuming task which demanded all he had to give, and his labour was much blessed by God. Paul's many letters give an indication of his qualities as a teacher. It must have been wonderful to receive instruction from him as he fulfilled this part of his ambition!

PRAYER
> We thank you, Lord, for Paul,
> The man whose life you turned around;
> And who, in love and mercy found
> That you are all-in-all.
> Whose sole ambition then became
> To add fresh glory to your name.

Free – from Personal Ambition (2)

Colossians 1:24–29

'We train everyone . . . in order to set everyone before God mature in Christ; I labour for that end, striving for it with the divine energy which is a power within me. Striving? Yes . . . (vv. 1:28–2:1, JM).

Paul's energy levels and ability to concentrate on the task in hand were, to say the least, remarkable. Indeed, he had the capacity to keep a number of projects moving at the same time. Even so, his work with the churches, although immense in vision and activity, was not easily done. Our key verses give some indication of the drive and initiative exercised in his wide-ranging ministries. The Greek word which stands behind the word James Moffatt translates as 'striving' and which the NIV translates as 'struggling' gives us our English word 'agony'. W.E. Vine tells us that Paul used the same word of those who strive for mastery in the public games (*1 Cor 9:25 AV*); used it also in the sense of contending perseveringly against opposition and temptation (*1 Tim 6:11 NIV*), and of wrestling in prayer (*Col 4:12 NIV*). Our Lord used the same word when he told Pilate, 'My kingdom is not of this world. If it were, my servants would fight to prevent my arrest by the Jews' (*John 18:36 NIV*).

Paul laboured and strove for Christ because it was the great aim of his life to do so. He had no personal ambitions: all he wanted was to serve his Master. Whatever it cost him physically or spiritually he was willing to give. He considered himself to have no life outside Christ: 'For to me', he said, 'to live is Christ and to die is gain' (*Phil 1:21 NIV; cf. Gal 2:20*).

We take note also of the energy which worked so strongly within him because it was the resurrection power of Christ (*cf. Eph 1:19,20*). Christ's power was always at work striving to achieve his Father's will and it is reasonable, therefore, to assume that the same power in people will have the same aim.

PRAYER

Mould my ambition, Lord, to serve but you,
Help me to concentrate upon your will,
To let your will prevail in all I do,
And all you plan for me, Lord, to fulfil.
Come, occupy the central place in me,
For I would serve but you, exclusively.

Free – to be a Slave

Romans 1:1–6

'Paul, a servant [slave] of Christ Jesus' (v. 1a, NIV).

The translators have softened the original word for servant because it actually means 'slave'. Of that original word W.E. Vine says that it is 'an adjective signifying "in bondage" '; Joseph H. Thayer clarifies it as, 'to make a slave of, reduce to bondage'. Had Paul meant that he was a servant of Christ in the less-stark sense of being a slave, he would probably have made it abundantly clear. Through the gospel he was free in every sense of that word, and he chose to be Christ's slave. It was a role he cherished because it was exactly what he wanted to be.

Paul, the young, dynamic, rising leader within Pharisaism, who so happily and efficiently initiated the first great persecution of Christians, surrendered his leadership role to become the slave of the same Lord he had fought by attacking his followers (*Acts 9:1–5*). By surrendering his rights to himself, Paul discovered that he was appointed by his Master to be a leader on a world stage because Jesus called him to become an apostle – the apostle to the Gentiles (Gal 2:7,8). Paul could not foresee it, but his enslavement to Christ resulted in his name becoming one of the most honoured and influential in all history.

In the early days of his discipleship Paul realised that all the time he had considered himself to be a free man he was, in fact, in bondage to sin (7:23). It was his new life in Christ that made him free and, the moment he was free, he chose to be the bond-slave of his Redeemer. He was wise to do so.

Not at any time in the days ahead did he lose sight of this bond-slave relationship with his Master. He actually extended the idea considering himself to be a slave to all if by so doing he could win as many as possible to Christ (*1 Cor 9:19*).

PRAISE

A slave of Christ!
Is there a greater occupation?
To serve the King of kings –
A perfect, glorious vocation!
To love and serve him and his word obey –
Life has no greater joy, no better way.

Free – to be Powerful

Ephesians 3:7–13

'I became a servant of this gospel by the gift of God's grace given me through the working of his power' (v. 7, NIV).

In one way or another, the word power is in constant use in Paul's letters, as a glance at any concordance of the Bible indicates. Although many nuances of the power of God are revealed in Scripture, in our key verse power refers to the power of God as it acts upon the minds and hearts of people. Paul had no doubt: of himself he was weak, but his weakness led to strength because it thrust him back upon God and in sheer dependence he allowed the power of God to work through him (*2 Cor 12:7–10; cf. 13:4*). God does not spare his power; those who turn to him find that his power and resources are without limit (*Eph 3:20*).

Nothing erodes spiritual power more than entertaining negative emotions such as bitterness and doubt, or engaging in negative behaviour like compromise, prayerlessness, poor stewardship of time, of rejected opportunities for service, or just plain, ordinary sin. But Paul was free; he was striving with all his energy to be Christ's man and the channels of grace were unimpeded. Because of this, the divine power flowed into him.

What a man of power he was! Tradition has it that he was small and not particularly impressive in appearance. He was devoid of those physical endowments that give some leaders a powerful presence and an immediate impact on people, but he was a mighty man through whom God chose to speak with incredible power. To read the accounts of his journeys in the Acts of the Apostles, study the routes of his missionary travels, read his letters to the churches, is to be persuaded that here was no ordinary man, but a person in whom the power of God dwelt in abundance. A man of exceptional energy might have covered as much ground, but the divine power within Paul ensured that his work would last.

PRAYER

It is for power, O Lord, I plead;
Power to meet my soul's great need,
Power to witness in your name,
Power to set dull hearts aflame.
Your resurrection power to me, Lord, give,
That to your glory I might daily live.

Free – to be Powerful in Prayer

Acts 27:1-44 (13–26)

'So keep up your courage, men, for I have faith in God that it will happen just as he told me' (v. 25, NIV).

The apostle's journeyings must always have been bathed in prayer. Although he suffered much for the sake of the gospel (*2 Cor 11:23–33*), he was spared many of the dangers and hazards that must have beset any traveller on those long, often lonely roads, as he moved from one centre to another. Every day was an answer-to-prayer day. That he was powerful in prayer can be illustrated from a variety of events in his life but, because of the sheer immediacy of the problems he faced, we refer to his journey to Rome, and the storm in the Mediterranean Sea.

When Paul told the centurion about of the disaster that would overtake them if they continued their journey (*vv. 9–12*), he must have done so from guidance received in his prayers. As a non-seaman, he had no experience, except that of prayer, on which to draw. Conscious of the dangers facing them, Paul must have been much in prayer during the voyage and when, after his advice had been ignored and they were caught in the storm, he had an authoritative message for them. All was going to be well with the passengers and crew although the ship would founder (*vv. 21–26*). Prayer must have been the source of his confidence also, when he insisted that the crew should remain with the ship and that all 276 people on board would be saved (*vv. 30–38*).

We note, too, that when everyone had landed safely and Paul's party were enjoying the hospitality of Publius, the island's chief official, Paul's gift of healing was used. This power came to him after prayer, and he healed Publius and the 'rest of the sick on the island' (*28:7–9*). The fact that Paul's channels of communication with God were clear, meant that his prayers were practical and powerful insofar as they were answered.

PRAYER

> Come, my soul, thy suit prepare,
> Jesus loves to answer prayer;
> He himself has bid thee pray,
> Therefore will not say thee nay.

(John Newton, SASB 563)

The First Sunday in Advent

Isaiah 11:1–5

A shoot will come up from the stump of Jesse; from his roots a Branch will bear fruit' (v. 1, NIV).

As the history of Israel rolled on in its troubled way – troubled because of political intrigue, dreams of conquest and experience of disaster, spiritual blindness and moral decline – God kept in touch with his people through the prophets. We stand in awe of those men of God who, living in times of faithlessness and impending tragedy, kept faith with God at whose command they lit candles of hope for the nation (*Isa 7:10–17; 9:2–7; WoL Advent 98*). Now, at this Advent Season, we return to Isaiah who strengthened the Messianic hope with the prophecy of a shoot from the stump of Jesse, and a *Branch* – note the capital letter indicating the Messiah – which will bear fruit.

William Wilson gives the meaning of the Hebrew word for *Branch* as, 'a slip, scion, or young sucker of a tree, selected and reserved for planting; a descendant of a family: Isa 11:1, of the Messiah'. We have no difficulty in understanding why Isaiah was either given, or chose to use, this word for Jesus.

Implicit in the metaphor of the Branch is the fact that Israel's past, which was less worthy than God had wanted, would not be wasted: the Messiah would be linked with it. Israel's failures would not be ignored, nor would the promises God had made to them. In fact, the future, centred around the Messiah, would grow out of their past. David was the greatest of Israel's kings, and the Messiah would, on the human level, be of his line (*Matt 1:1–17; cf. Rom 1:3 NEB, REB*). Israel's past, like most human experience, though marred by rebellion would not be wasted. This prophecy assured Israel, and assures us also, of that.

PRAYER
> God does not cut his losses with mankind,
>   His love continues steadfast to the end;
> With tenderness he holds us in his mind,
>   A privilege we cannot comprehend.
> It was because he loved that Jesus came,
> Our broken lives to heal and souls reclaim.

PRAYER SUBJECT   *For despairing people to find hope.*

Free – to be Powerful in Faith

Acts 13:1–5

'The two of them, sent on their way by the Holy Spirit, went down to Seleucia and sailed from there to Cyprus' (v. 4, NIV).

So began one of the most momentous journeys the world has ever known. Two men, called and equipped by the Holy Spirit, embarked on a mission that was the direct cause of the spread of the gospel across the world, and would bless all future generations. It is true that they were not without contacts, because their Jewish heritage gave them access to synagogues. This afforded them a starting point in most cities, but that does not diminish their spirit of adventure nor the immensity of their faith.

The world of that day was awash with religions of many kinds; but Christianity was not just another religion that could be accommodated like the rest. He or she who accepted Christ was required to reject those religions, a rejection which gave solid grounds for opposition of one form or another. Every day required the exercise of faith, every journey was a step in faith, and Paul was found equal to the demands. If ever a New Testament hall of heroes of the faith was erected, Paul, and those associated with him, would be found in the places of highest honour.

In cultures of moral darkness: perversion, sorcery (*v. 8; 19:18,19*) and viciousness (*14:19,20*) this man Paul, powerful in faith and prayer, lit the flame of the gospel and the flame grew and spread. Even when they had to leave a city quickly because of riots organised against them, Paul's faith did not waver; he went on to plant other churches (*17:5–15*) and the kingdom of our Lord continued to prosper. Nor did his example or counsel falter as time passed. From prison where, surely, his faith was tested, he wrote to Timothy, his companion on many of his adventures (*16:1–5*), 'Fight the good fight of the faith' (*1 Tim 6:12*). It is a counsel we can accept for ourselves.

PRAYER
Things deemed impossible I dare,
Thine is the call and thine the care;
Thy wisdom shall the way prepare,
Thy will be done.

(*Frederick Mann, SASB* 744)

Free – to be Fruitful

Acts 9:10–19

'I will show him how much he must suffer for my name' (v. 16, NIV).

The amazement of Ananias at the instruction given him to go and meet Saul of Tarsus for the purpose of healing him, is perfectly understandable. His composure also, in obeying the Lord's command is utterly commendable. But then, why should he, or any one else be surprised at the actions of God who calls whom he will to do his work? No one is good enough by nature to merit such trust, which means that God will always be taking into partnership unlikely people, among whom we, too, are numbered.

After his lengthy period of preparation (*cf. Gal 2:1*) Paul was launched on his life's work of evangelism, pastoring and teaching. The Spirit of Christ had made him free in order to bear fruit of the most remarkable kind. It was not only that he planted new churches, but that he had the will and the skill to nurture them (*15:36*), and he continued to feed them with his highly-inspirational letters. What a large number of gifts he possessed and with what outstanding commitment he used them!

Let one illustration of his fruitfulness and influence suffice, that of Ephesus. Paul did not begin the church at Ephesus (*18:19, 20; 19:1ff.*) but he certainly established it and remained there for a period of three years (*20:31*). Towards the end of his third missionary journey Paul wanted to meet the Ephesian elders and, because his ship did not call at Ephesus, the elders travelled to Miletus to see him. The account of this meeting reveals just how fruitful Paul's years with them had been (*20:1ff*). From beginning to end, his faith, prayers and work (*cf. Eph 1:15–23; 2:14–22*) had nourished them in Christ, and they loved him in return (*Acts 20:36–38*). It must be true that Paul's life illustrates our Lord's teaching, 'If a man remains in me and I in him, he will bear much fruit' (*John 15:5b*).

PRAYER

  You make your people fruitful, Lord,
   You give the vision and the call,
  The needed grace, the inspiring word;
   You simply ask that we give all.
  And we, whom you redeemed from shame,
  Bear fruit and glorify your name.

Free – to Receive (1)

1 Corinthians 15:1–11

'For what I received I passed on to you as of first importance'
(v. 3a, NIV).

Paul went on to describe what it was that he had received (*vv. 3–8*) and this brief statement constitutes one of the earliest creeds of the Church. As the account states, it is a creed of 'first importance'. This chapter is part of Paul's letter to the Corinthians because some Corinthians were experiencing doctrinal problems and he wanted to correct their views. Without that correction, their faith would have had a faulty foundation.

We take note of the fact that, although Paul was an original thinker with a massive capacity to follow through the implications of a divine revelation, he accepted the creed totally. By the quality of his acceptance he was able to build on it and develop further inspired lines of thought, of the same quality as other inspired thoughts shown in this letter (*see 1:20–30*). Paul's commitment to Christ and his gospel ensured that he had no reservations about the fundamentals of the apostolic faith. The Church had come to its basic beliefs prayerfully and by the guidance of the Holy Spirit. Paul might well be concerned over priority issues such as that discussed by the Council of Jerusalem (*Acts 15:1–29*), but the death and Resurrection of Jesus were of prime importance. Any wavering would weaken the foundations on which the Church is built, and Paul did not waver.

As we scan the life of Paul, we observe just how consistently he presented the historic faith. Although he lacked the apostolic experience of witnessing our Lord's earthly ministry (*1:21,22*), Paul was no less convinced of the Incarnation of Jesus than the other apostles (*cf. Rom 1:2–4*) and presented Christ as Son of man and Son of God with enormous conviction (*Phil 2:5–11*). On the basis of this creed of 'first importance' Paul proceeded to build some of the great doctrines of the Church.

PRAYER   *The Church believes in Jesus Christ,*
            The Son of God once sacrificed,
            Once raised triumphant from the dead,
            And made of heaven and earth the head.
            This is the creed the Church received:
            The creed we have with joy believed.

Free – to Receive (2)

Galatians 1:11–24

'I want you to know, brothers, that the gospel I preached is not something that man made up. I did not receive it from any man, nor was I taught it; rather, I received it by revelation from Jesus Christ' (vv. 11,12, NIV).

Our key verse today seems to be in conflict with our key verse of yesterday but, obviously, there is a way whereby they can be seen to complement, rather than contradict, each other. As we discovered earlier (*WoL 22 23 Sept 95*), Paul's ministry and, indeed, the very basis of the gospel was being challenged and his letter to the people of Galatia is his defence. We are glad he had the problem because the defence is so helpful to us!

As we know, Paul was nurtured in the Jewish faith. From childhood he had been subjected to the teaching of Judaism: he had learned their traditions, how to interpret Scripture in the Rabbinic way, had learned their rituals, the nuances of their Jewishness. Almost everything he knew had come through other people (*v. 14*). But it was not so with his Christian faith – this he had learned from Christ. As the other apostles had listened to Jesus during his earthly ministry, Paul had listened to the risen Lord in the loneliness of Arabia (*vv. 15–17*). His freedom in Christ enabled him to receive the revelations Jesus wanted to impart. With Christ as his mentor, it is not surprising that the truths he had received matched those of Peter and James, whom he did not meet for quite a long time (*vv. 18,19*).

Following his time in Jerusalem (*v. 18*), and because Paul's personal revelations coincided with the foundational beliefs of the Church, he was able to affirm the creed as of 'first importance' (*1 Cor 15:3*). It is a belief that stands as the foremost fact of faith, given to new Christians for acceptance and guidance, and passed on from one generation to the next.

PRAYER   *I thank you, Lord, for creeds which guide and bless:*
And thank you too, because you speak to me,
Disclose to me part of the mystery
Of who I am, and of your righteousness.
I treasure all these revelations new
Which bring me so much closer, Lord, to you.

Free – to Receive (3)

Galatians 1:11–24

'I want you to know, brothers, that the gospel I preached is not something that man made up. I did not receive it from any man, nor was I taught it; rather, I received it by revelation from Jesus Christ' (vv. 11, 12, NIV).

We cannot all be like Paul: he had his own calling, gifts and role, but one of the significant lessons for us to learn from him is that his freedom in Christ enabled him to live up to his capacity. Such was his dedication that he allowed nothing to stand between him and his Master. Whatever Christ asked of him he gave and, whatever his Master gave to him, he received.

In spite of all his gifts, and they were both numerous and splendid, the main reason for the quality of the insights we find in his letters must surely be that he had an amazing sensitivity towards Christ. His communion was rich and unbroken: doubts, self-will, unconfessed sins did not block the channels of communication and his freedom in the gospel left him free to receive all that Jesus had to give. We thank God he was free to receive, because that enabled him to be free to give.

Almost everything he wrote or, indeed, that is recorded of him can be taken as an illustration of this freedom to receive. Who can compute the blessings, for instance, he received and proceeded to share with the Romans and, through his letter to them, the entire Church? From that extraordinary letter we note how Paul proceeds from his exposition on 'justification by faith' (*Rom 5:1ff.*) to the life the Spirit imparts (*Rom 8:1–27*), and then moves us, with powerful truths and majestic words, about the blessings of God's care for us (*Rom 8:28–34*). As though that were not enough, he provides us with the inspiring climax that in all things we are more than conquerors, and that nothing can separate us from the love of Christ (*Rom 8:35–39*). What a blessing Paul's sensitivity to God has been to us all!

TO PONDER
> *You speak to me, O Lord, in many ways;*
> *Through revelations given to other minds,*
> *Through hymns expressive of our nobler days,*
> *A special insight which its target finds,*
> *But, best of all, you speak direct to me,*
> *And by your word, you set my spirit free.*

Free – to be an Example

2 Timothy 1:3–14

'What you heard from me, keep as the pattern of sound teaching, with faith and love in Christ Jesus' (v. 13, NIV).

It was not immodesty that made Paul refer, on a number of occasions, to the importance of example (*cf. Wol 8 July 99*). Three times he told the Corinthians that they were to follow his example (*1 Cor 4:16; 7:7; 11:1*); twice he encouraged the Philippians to imitate him (*Phil 3:17;4:9*); once he told the Thessalonians to follow him and, we note, others of his group (*2 Thess 3:7*). Then, as our key verse indicates, he proposed himself as the young Timothy's pattern for ministry (*v. 13*).

The freedom Paul enjoyed because he lived in the Spirit (*cf. Gal 5:22–26*) enabled him to present himself to people as an example to follow. His life in the Spirit of Christ was not an opportunity to magnify himself, or create the impression that he was superior to other people (*Eph 3:7,8; Phil 2:3, 4;1 Tim 1:12–16*). He knew so well, as all saints know, that the nearer you are to our Lord, the less worthy you feel yourself to be.

We note that whereas in other exhortations to follow him, the context suggests that Paul was emphasising a behavioural pattern; with Timothy he was stressing the need to follow him in his suffering and teaching. As with a number of Paul's letters this letter to Timothy was written from prison (*vv. 8,16; 2:9*) and he was expecting martyrdom (*4:6–8*), but he wrote with his usual faith and fortitude – he knew there were worse things than martyrdom (*4:16–18*). It is true that not all Christians are called upon to suffer for their faith, even though suffering can never be ruled out, but the faith, that body of truth on which Christianity is founded, the 'deposit' as the NIV puts it (*v. 14*), is crucial to us all. If we follow Paul, as he followed Christ (*1 Cor 11:1*), we will do well.

PRAYER
We all set patterns, Lord,
    In ways we do not realise,
By manner or by word
    By foolish acts or wise.
O help us, Lord, to say and do
Those words and things that point to you.

The Second Sunday in Advent

Isaiah 11:1–5

'A shoot will come up from the stump of Jesse; from his roots a Branch will bear fruit' (v. 1, NIV).

Towards the end of his book, *A History of Israel*, John Bright wrote, 'The destination of Old Testament history and theology is Christ and his gospel.' No doubt, there are people who would disagree with John Bright's contention, but, without Jesus, to Christian eyes there appears to be much fortitude and little cheer in the Old Testament. With Jesus, however, the Old Testament and the experience of the Jewish people cohere perfectly.

A new branch on a tree is a sign of hope; it hints at the unlimited possibilities of new growth and fruitful abundance. And this Messianic sign, the Branch from the stump of Jesse, quickens hope also. In a nation which was staggering under its burdens, the result of its alienation from God, the prophet's word told those who had 'ears to hear', that God was interested still in reclamation. They remained part of his plans for the world (*cf. Gen 12:3b*), and the day would come, said the prophet, when 'the Root of Jesse will stand as a banner for the peoples; the nations will rally to him' (*11:10*).

If we need a reminder that hope is justifiable in our world today, we have that reminder as we celebrate Advent. God promised the new Branch from the stump of Jesse (*v. 1*) and, as we read history, we see how gloriously fruitful that Branch has been and is still. This prophecy made to a Jerusalem in turmoil has proved itself true in every generation since the Incarnation of Jesus. His fruitfulness is evident on every continent; his influence continues to grow as the hopeless become hope-full and Christ is acclaimed as Lord and King.

PRAISE

Above our sad and wilful world
*   Christ's loving banner flies unfurled.*
It tells of sin's enormous cost,
*   The price he paid to save the lost,*
And tells that hope is not in vain
Since he, the Christ, is here to reign.

PRAYER SUBJECT   *Victims of violence in the home.*

Growing in Grace

1 Corinthians 12:27–31 (following 31.7.99)

'Eagerly desire the greater gifts' (v. 31, NIV).

We return to the apostle Paul and his explanation of the gifts which the Holy Spirit gives to God's people. The list is not complete (*cf. Rom 12:6–8*) because Paul was dealing with a specific situation in Corinth. Perhaps our changing world will ensure that the list of gifts will never be complete, but Paul was stressing to the Corinthians that their own personal list of gifts need not be regarded as complete either.

As we grow in grace we grow in capacity: there is nothing static about the Christian life and the Holy Spirit is constantly at work within us. Faithfulness in the use of our gifts leads to greater opportunities (*cf. Matt 25:14–29*) which, surely, leads to greater giftedness. Furthermore, it is the experience of many Christians that, as they have been thrust into new and more demanding situations, the Holy Spirit has, wisely and generously, met the new demands with the appropriate gifts.

One Greek word only stands behind 'eagerly desire' (*v. 31a*) and that Greek word means 'to burn with zeal, desire earnestly, to pursue'. It expresses the intention of the Holy Spirit to make each one of us bear more fruit for the Master (*cf. John 15:1–8*), and the word reflects also our aspirations because we want to be more profitable; we are reluctant to stagnate, to allow the years to diminish our enthusiasm and usefulness.

It is not in the nature of love to settle for the least, or of freedom in the Lord to be listless and low-key. Christ has done so much for us that we cannot do enough for him and his cause. That being so, we 'earnestly desire the greater gifts'.

TO PONDER

> *If we desire the best, who knows*
> *To what extent potential grows,*
> *Or how our faith's tenacity*
> *Develops our capacity.*
> *The more we do, the more achieve,*
> *The more we ask, the more receive.*
> *God has within his treasure store,*
> *More gifts for those who ask for more.*

The Most Excellent Way

1 Corinthians 12:31b–13:3

'But eagerly desire the greater gifts. And now I will show you the most excellent way (v. 31, NIV).

We marvel at Paul's ability to express the mysteries of God so clearly. He was not only a great thinker, he was a great communicator; his words are alive still with the energy of God so that after nearly two thousand years he continues to encourage the people of God. Not many theologians can lift and inspire their readers, but Paul rarely fails to do so. When he is overwhelmed by the truths which flood his heart and mind, the Holy Spirit seems to dominate him and he begins to express the divine thoughts in a most powerful and memorable way. 'Paul', said James Moffatt, 'was a theologian who had a vein of poetry'; it is an attribute which has enriched the world immensely.

The love to which Paul refers in this remarkable chapter is a particular kind of love. It is distinct from romantic love, brotherly love, the love of friends or community; rather, it is the love God himself possesses and displays towards his Son and all mankind, and is the love we are to have within us (*John 17:26*). In attempting to define Christian love, W.E. Vine said it 'is not an impulse from the feelings, it does not always run with the natural inclinations, nor does it spend itself only upon those with whom some affinity is found. Love seeks the welfare of all and works no ill to anyone.' This, above all, is the love Christ commands us to have (*John 15:12; WoL 26 June 98*).

Love is the 'most excellent way' because love alone has the interests of everyone, including God, at heart. It is a love which not only produces solutions but initiates harmony, even healing if that be necessary. More importantly, since this kind of love is the way God has chosen to be his way of working, no other method can be its equal.

TO PONDER *Love has a language, all its own making,*
Voiced in its giving, love gives its best;
Instant and constant with joy whilst awaking,
Tells its own story – love stands the test.

(Joseph Buck, SASB 51)

If

1 Corinthians 13:1–3

'If I speak in the tongues of men and of angels, but have not love, I am only a resounding gong or a clanging cymbal' (v. 1, NIV).

How or where this chapter of Scripture is read, whether at a wedding, ordination or simply for pleasure, it is a means of grace, but Paul intended it to be read in the context of spiritual gifts. The Corinthians had a number of problems, one of which was that they were disunited (*1:10*) and even their gifts, which were meant to unite them, became a cause of division, because some gifts were valued more than others (*cf. 12:14–26*).

The emphasis the Corinthians gave to these gifts indicated that the spirit of love was not very evident among them, hence this glorious chapter on the subject of love. Paradoxically, we can almost be glad that the problem existed because, without it, we would not have had this beautiful 'hymn to love'.

Paul had often seen devotees of the gods, Dionysus and Cybele, walk through the streets beating gongs and banging cymbals. Both as a Jew and Christian, the apostle would dismiss such parades as noisy witnesses to false religions, and it was with those irrelevant noises he compared one of the most coveted spiritual gifts, if that gift was not being lovingly exercised. 'If I speak in the tongues of men and of angels, but have not love, I am a resounding gong or clanging cymbal' (*v. 1*).

The gift of tongues was an impressive gift because it was the evidence of divine favour. How could people, they argued, speak like that except God had blessed them with this gift? Others, not so gifted, could be forgiven for looking on with envy because, by the same reasoning, they were unblessed. Even so, said Paul in effect, be your eloquence the eloquence of the angels, if you are unloving, it is worth no more than a pagan cymbal.

PRAYER

> *If I speak with an angel's tongue*
> *If through me are new dreams begun,*
> *If my eloquence sounds divine,*
> *And God uses me as a sign,*
> *That only is true, that only can be,*
> *If love, his pure love, is dwelling in me.*

So Much and so Little

1 Corinthians 13:1–3

'If I have the gift of prophecy ... but have not love, I am nothing'
(v. 2, NIV).

We ought not to underestimate the importance of prophecy to the apostle Paul. When he used the term he was not emphasising the aspect of prophecy which reveals that on a distant date some important event is going to take place. Rather, he would have in his mind the fact that the prophet was a person steeped in the word of God; someone who lived so close to God that he or she could relate that word to here-and-now people and situations. Through the exercise of the gift of prophecy God could be recognised as a present reality who ought to be honoured and worshipped in his own right (*cf. 14:24,25*).

Although prophecy was not the only gift Paul used as he travelled the world, it was a major gift. Without it, he could not have communicated the will of God with such power and effectiveness. We must remember, also, that Paul was nurtured in the Jewish faith. Although he was an expert in the history and law of his nation (*cf. Rom 4:1ff.*), he had studied the prophets (*cf. 14:21*) and been enormously influenced by them. He knew their value to God and knew that a ministry of that kind was required in the Church. Prophecy was important to the apostle.

Even so, he believed that it was possible to be a prophet and, because of the absence of love, be an ineffective witness to the counsels of God. 'If I have the gift of prophecy ... but have not love, I am nothing' (*v. 2*). Perhaps the high-profile role of the prophet produces its own temptations and rewards; it is possible, for instance, to feed on a generously given respect and lose sight of the servant element in discipleship. But Paul was as clear as he was uncompromising: great though the gift may be, love is the all-important ingredient.

TO PONDER
Though in declaring Christ to the sinner,
I may all men surpass,
If love impassioned seal not the message,
I am nought but sounding brass.

(*Arch R. Wiggins, SASB 530*)

Even More!

1 Corinthians 13:1–3

'If I . . . can fathom all mysteries and all knowledge, and if I have a faith that can move mountains, but have not love, I am nothing' (v. 2, NIV).

In any society a person who seems to have a sure touch in revealing the mysteries of God, whether that person is genuine or false, will not lack for a congregation. Our world has always been fascinated by the spiritual world and welcoming to those who claim the power to unlock its mysteries. In like manner, a special place is afforded people whose store of knowledge, spiritual or otherwise, is impressive. Paul remains definite, however: without love, such revelations count for little.

From the more passive exercise of revealing spiritual insights and knowledge, Paul moved to the people who are among life's great achievers: the people who possess the gift of faith. That is the gift that enables men and women to overcome enormous odds in order to turn a great vision into a reality. It will be recalled that Jesus spoke of a faith that can move mountains (*cf. Matt 21:21*). Again, although the faith expressed may be impressive, an absence of love devalues it. Only love, the divine love in people, fulfils God's great purposes.

If we reflect upon the fact that some unloving people have apparently achieved much and, as we look more closely at Paul's words, we note that he says 'If I . . . have not love, *I* am nothing'. Perhaps we ought to be remembering that we can be a conduit of divine power and grace (*cf. Phil 1:15–18*) and still miss the prize God has for those who run his race (*9:24–27*). And did not our Lord have special words for people who, under the guise of serving God were serving their own ends? Of such people he said, 'I tell you the truth, they have received their reward in full' (*Matt 6:2,5,16*). In this sense, Paul's words, 'If I . . . have not love, I am nothing', echo the words of his Master.

TO PONDER
> *Though I have wisdom lighting all mysteries;*
> *Though I may all things know;*
> *Though great my faith be, removing mountains,*
> *Without love, 'tis empty show.*

(*Arch R. Wiggins, SASB 530*)

Total Sacrifice

1 Corinthians 13:1–3

'If I give all I possess to the poor and surrender my body to the flames, but have not love, I gain nothing' (v. 3, NIV).

In this hymn, this lyric to love, Paul moves on an ascending scale. He commences with eloquence and moves through a list of impressive and crucial gifts in which he indicates how these gifts are not only subordinate to love but, that without love, they are of little worth. With the skill of a superlative communicator, Paul climaxed this section of his poem by referring to sacrifices of the highest order: 'If I give all I possess to the poor . . . but have not love, I gain nothing'.

One of Paul's great friends was Barnabas (*Acts 11:25,26*), and Paul would know that in the early days of the Church Barnabas sold a field 'and brought the money and put it all at the apostles' feet' (*Acts 4:32–37*). Barnabas and others who engaged in this act of generosity, did so out of love. But Paul knew that it was possible to make such sacrificial gestures for other motives and, if the motive was other than love, the giver had gained nothing. It is not possible to buy the favours of God.

From the sacrifice of material resources, Paul moved to the ultimate sacrifice, namely, that of one's life. Would anyone sacrifice his or her life for less than love? In Athens there was a tomb of a man who had jumped on to a burning pyre; the inscription on the tomb, which he himself had prepared, said, 'Zarmano-chegas . . . made himself immortal and lies here'. It is possible to go to one's death for reasons of pride, a misplaced zeal, a belief that martyrdom wins a special favour from God. But whatever other motive may drive a man to make this, the greatest sacrifice, even so, said Paul, 'If I . . . surrender my body to the flames, but have not love, I gain nothing.' God looks for love, because he is a God of love.

PRAYER

I must love thee, love must rule me,
Springing up and flowing forth
From a childlike heart within me,
Or my work is nothing worth.

(*Albert Orsborn, SASB 522*)

The Third Sunday in Advent

Isaiah 11:1–5

'A shoot will come up from the stump of Jesse; from his roots a Branch will bear fruit' (v. 1, NIV).

In his prophecy concerning the coming of the Messiah, Isaiah was quite sure that the coming king would be well equipped to fulfil his tremendous task. Not only would he be born of the royal line, the dynasty of David, but he would be endowed with the Spirit of God and all the gifts he needed.

We note that the Spirit of God would rest on him. In this context, the meaning of rest is to abide in, to settle down; all the connotations were those of permanence (*v. 2a*). As the prophecy proceeds we observe with interest the way in which the qualities or attributes mentioned will be exercised. Because of his wisdom and understanding (*v. 2b*), he will not judge superficially but always with an eye on the righteousness of God (*vv. 3b,4a*). His skill in counselling (*v. 2c*) will enable him to dispense justice for the poor and needy (*v. 4a*). The Messiah's gift of power (*v. 2c*) marks him out as a supernatural being. None but God could 'strike the earth with the rod of his mouth . . . and slay the wicked' (*v. 4b*). King David, also of the root of Jesse, was a great king but human frailty diminished him; not so the Branch, the Messiah: 'Righteousness will be his belt and faithfulness the sash round his waist' (*v. 5*).

Israel could look forward with hope and a growing confidence that God was going to do something new (*43:19*) and, clearly, many people had that hope. They are represented by Simeon and Anna (*Luke 2:25–38*) and those who welcomed Jesus (*Luke 8:40*). We celebrate the fact that their hope and confidence was justified; that Jesus came and, having come, is with us still.

PRAYER
What wonderful provision you have made
For those who have the courage to believe;
Through Christ we have no cause to be afraid,
Since all we need, from him we can receive.
And through the Christ our lives have been fulfilled,
Which from the first, O Lord, is what you willed.

PRAYER SUBJECT *Lonely, hurting people.*

Love is Patient

1 Corinthians 13:4–7

'Love is patient, love is kind' (v. 4a, NIV).

It was courageous of Paul to embark upon a description of the behaviour expected of those who follow the Lord Jesus. As the acknowledged leader of the churches outside of Israel, his own behaviour would be measured by the standards he set so powerfully for everyone in this remarkable 'love' chapter. His words provide for us a description, not exhaustive of course, of our Lord himself. The Christ never failed to show the characteristics Paul declared to be the required behaviour of the believer.

Love is patient. Paul himself knew much about the divine patience. He never lost sight of the way in which he had behaved towards the followers of Jesus (*Acts 9:1,2; 22:3–5; 26:9–11*), and must have meditated long on the divine patience. We ourselves do not find it hard to remember the period before we surrendered to Christ. Our wilfulness led us into many wrong paths and we did many wrong things in consequence. Even so, the divine patience was exercised in our favour and forgiveness was granted to us without hesitation or recrimination. No doubt we would continue to confess our indebtedness to the patience of God as we have continued with our discipleship. So many foolish things, childish attitudes, mean-spirited words have marked our pilgrimage that, but for the patience of God, we would have been cast aside as worthless long ago.

Although we have been dealt with patiently, we know how hard it is sometimes to be patient towards others. Some people seem destined to exasperate us with their ability to misunderstand us and say all the wrong things but 'love is patient', and we have no option but to treat them with the patience God has exercised towards us. More people have been won for the Master through the patience of the saints than through their impatience.

TO PONDER
Now the fruit of the Spirit is patience,
    And the fruit of the Spirit is peace,
  The fruit of the Spirit is gentleness
    And joy that will never cease.

(John Gowans, SASB Chorus 46)

Love is Kind

1 Corinthians 13:4–7

'Love is patient, love is kind. It does not envy, it does not boast, it is not proud' (v. 4, NIV).

Patience (*WoL 13 Dec 99*) and kindness go together (*cf. Gal 5:22*); it is difficult to see how one can exist without the other but, although linked, they each have their own distinctive characteristics. Kindness is gentleness, benevolence, warmth and affection. A truly kind person is more rare than should be the case. The kindness, however, of which Paul writes is more than just a benevolent and gentle disposition; it is goodness in action, love expressed in deeds, because love is not merely passive it is active. Love has eyes to see a need and take the steps required to ensure that the need is met. Love is for ever going the extra mile and doing it with a sense of joy and privilege. Wise, perceptive, even shrewd though the kind person is, he or she is never guilty of hasty judgments or hurtful speech.

Envy seemed to be a problem with the Corinthians, largely because they had set a value scale in spiritual gifts and, to them, certain gifts were a source of envy. The problem is not exclusively Corinthian: envy is present in most communities and, so often, the success of one is the envy of another. The only antidote to the corrosive influence of envy is love. If we love, we share another's joys and achievements. Neither does love boast. To catalogue and parade our successes is damaging to ourselves and injurious to others. Immodesty has nothing to do with kindness or reality: in the first place it hurts those whose achievements are less and, in the second place, it does not acknowledge the fact that others may have achieved more.

Love is not proud: the translation 'puffed up' (*AV*) better describes this condition than 'proud'. Because it is un-Christlike, there is no place for arrogance or conceit in love.

PRAYER

Spirit of God, now dwell in me,
And let my spirit loving be;
All selfish elements destroy,
Your love be both my aim and joy.
And let my life unconsciously display
Your love controlling me from day to day.

Love is not . . .

1 Corinthians 13:4–7

'It is not rude, it is not self-seeking, it is not easily angered, it keeps no record of wrongs' (v. 5, NIV).

Rudeness is dismissive, unkind and hurtful, and ought never to be part of the Christian's weaponry in handling other people. Our lives are to be marked by love. Churlishness, ingratitude, sarcasm, and violence of speech are not to be part of our lifestyle. Love is not like that, neither is it self-seeking. One of the aims of love is not self-aggrandisement but, rather, seeking to advantage other people. The Christian life should reveal the life of our Lord which was characterised by self-giving. In the Acts of the Apostles (*20:35 NIV*), Paul used a statement of Jesus which is not recorded elsewhere, 'It is more blessed to give than to receive'. Experience confirms the truth of that.

The patience and kindness of love ensure that we are not easily angered. Tempers with 'short fuses' or an inability to suffer fools, are dispositions Christians cannot afford. A moment's reflection would tell us that there must be reasons why an unwise statement has been made or action taken. Furthermore, not many situations are improved by an eruption of anger. Elsewhere, Paul seems to make provision for righteous anger – 'Be angry but do not sin' – but the occasions for such anger must be few. Even so, he added, 'give no opportunity to the devil' (*Eph 4:26 RSV*). Love does not easily give way to anger.

Love 'keeps no record of wrongs'. It is so very easy to remember hurtful things and thoughtless deeds. It is also possible to read into words and deeds intentions which are not true, but a mental record of such wrongs festers and spreads its poison. 'Lord, how many times shall I forgive my brother' asked Peter, 'Up to seven times?' Jesus replied, 'I tell you, not seven times, but seventy-seven times' (*Matt 18:21,22 NIV*). By that time Peter would have lost count and would keep on forgiving!

PRAYER

Lord make me quick to see and quick to feel
The thoughtless word and deed that causes pain.
Let me by love and understanding heal
The wound that otherwise could long remain.
I would, Lord, like to have a caring mind
That is for ever loving, wise and kind.

Love – Limited and Limitless

1 Corinthians 13:4–7

'Love does not delight in evil but rejoices with the truth' (v. 6, NIV).

In addition to the other limits placed on love (*v. 5*), Paul, under the influence of the Holy Spirit, placed a further limitation – love does not delight in evil. The loving heart finds no pleasure in the downfall of another, no satisfaction in the knowledge that someone has been paid back in his own coin or got his just deserts. Neither does love pass on the details of another's misfortunes or sins unless, of course, it is for the benefit of harnessing prayer-power on that person's behalf.

'Love', continued the apostle, 'rejoices with the truth'. Of course we welcome the truth when it overcomes evil, lifts the cloud from a relationship, or simply puts the record straight. Occasionally, however, the truth can be uncomfortable. With typical insight William Barclay suggested that there may be times 'when it [truth] is the last thing we wish to hear'! Even so, if the truth helps us to be better people and better disciples, the pain of hearing it could turn soon to rejoicing.

The limitless nature of love is further emphasised with, 'love always protects, always trusts, always hopes, always endures' (*v. 7*). Presumably, the *NIV* translators took from the original Greek word the concept of a protective covering, a covering strong enough to 'bear all things' (*cf. NASB, AV*). The protection love gives is always that which is best for the individual and would never be a cover for immoral behaviour. Love has no difficulty in trusting God on the one hand, and trusting people on the other, even though on occasion that trust may be betrayed. In the long term that simple trust may prove to be redemptive. Love always hopes, believing that the worst of people can be changed by God's grace, and love never loses its power of endurance. When all else fails, love stands firm.

PRAYER
Help me, O Lord, your love to know,
And guilelessly your love to show.
Help me the weak and lost to shield,
With purpose unprepared to yield.
And let me trust in you implicitly,
In good times or in dark adversity.

Love Never Fails

1 Corinthians 13:8–13

'Love never fails. But where there are prophecies, they will cease; where there are tongues, they will be stilled' (v. 8a, NIV).

In this, his 'hymn to love', Paul was making more than a bold statement in the face of apparent evidence to the contrary that love, and love alone, would not fail. He knew that he had merited nothing less from God than judgment and death but, when he was confronted by Christ on the Damascus Road, he was met by the love of God as revealed through his Son (*Acts 9:1–6; Rom 5:5–8*), and Paul's heart was won by love. Thereafter, motivated by love, he sought to win others for his Master. It was with confidence, therefore, that he wrote, 'love never fails'.

Not that love's victories are easily won! Love bears its wounds as the risen Christ bears his (*John 20:26,27*), but love conquers, even if it means a Gethsemane or a Calvary, or both. Love has to be victorious because God is love and, great though the 'powers of this dark world' and 'the spiritual forces of evil in the heavenly realms' (*Eph 6:12*) may be, they cannot overwhelm the Almighty God. By their rejection of the love of God, people may deny themselves entry into his kingdom, but that is not love's failure, rather, it is the exercise of a freedom which, first and foremost, is a love-ordained gift.

Other things will fail. Prophecies will cease, tongues – that much envied gift in Corinth – will be stilled, and knowledge will pass away. All that is transient in human life, those vital as well as trivial things that differentiate earth from heaven will pass away. But love, eternal, unchanging and unconquerable, because it is the very essence of God, will remain.

PRAYER

Love suffereth patiently;
Love worketh silently;
*   Love seeketh not her own.*
Love never faileth;
Love still prevaileth,
Lord, in me thy love enthrone!

(Arch R. Wiggins, SASB 530)

The Prospect

1 Corinthians 13:8–13

'Now we see but a poor reflection as in a mirror; then we shall see face to face. Now I know in part; then I shall know fully, even as I am fully known' (v. 12, NIV).

Corinth was famous for many things, not least its production of mirrors. Since glass mirrors did not exist in Paul's day they were made of bronze which was highly polished to ensure as perfect as reflection as possible. Our text makes it clear that the reflection seen in the mirror is not the face of the beholder but, rather, is God, whom one day we will see 'face to face'. To help us understand this, commentators point to God's words to Aaron and Miriam in which he indicates that the prophets only had an imperfect view of him, 'But this is not true of my servant Moses . . . With him I speak face to face, clearly . . . he sees the form of God' (*Num 12:7–8*).

To those who have the will and the eyes to see, Paul's thought, therefore, is that reflected in life's mirror, is the picture of God as given by holy men. Seen also are the works of God; but the day will come when we will see him face to face. At present we see 'through a glass [mirror] darkly (*AV*), not fully comprehending all we see. as Paul added, 'Now I know in part; then, I shall know fully even as I am fully known'.

The prospect is glorious! Although our present understanding of God is stimulating and exciting, the reality ahead offers incredible experiences to us. Imperfect though our vision is, we trace, with confidence and joy, the ways of God in our lives. We may know a part only, but the part we know is marvellous! The providence of the Father, the redemptive work of Son and the continuing ministries of the Holy Spirit in our lives continue to delight and fulfil us. That God should offer more is, from his viewpoint reasonable, and from ours, marvellous.

PRAYER

> So in thy mercy make us wise,
>   And lead us in the ways of love,
> Until, at last, our wondering eyes
>   Look on thy glorious face above.

(*Arnold Thomas*)

The Fourth Sunday in Advent

Isaiah 11:1–5

'A shoot will come up from the stump of Jesse; from his roots a Branch will bear fruit' (v. 1, NIV).

For those who use *Words of Life* and have a non-Jewish background there may be something almost academic about this kind of preparation for the coming of Christ, as though we are reaching back into the Old Testament to find proof-texts to support our sense of history, and as though our assumption is that the Incarnation was the object of centuries of preparation. Some people might even feel that because our needs, rather than historical arguments, drove us to Christ, we have accepted, without undue stimulation, more or less everything that our teachers have told us.

For Jewish Christians, however, theirs is the sheer excitement of knowing that the Messiah was in the mind of God from the beginning. Their history, the law, the prophets are all fulfilled in him (*cf. Matt 5:17–20; 13:35*). Matthew was so persuaded of this that he commenced his Gospel with the genealogy of Jesus (*Matt 1:1–17*). He quoted also the prophets, 'He will be called a Nazarene' (*Matt 2:23*), because the root meaning of Nazarene and Nazareth is the same as 'the Branch'. To Jews who have become disciples of our Lord, the build-up to the Incarnation is revelation of the most remarkable order.

In the book, *The Witness of the Jews to God*, edited by David W. Torrance, Johanna-Ruth Dobschiner, under the heading of, *Christ, the Fulfilment of the Jewish Faith*, wrote, 'But Hallelujah, what brilliance of light, life and freedom, when the Messiah indeed proved himself alive, real and THE Truth: through him, our God became MY Father and I could speak with him, yes, as his child'. Clearly, Advent is celebration time!

PRAYER
> All praise, eternal Son, to thee
> Whose advent sets thy people free,
>   Whom with the Father, we adore,
>   And Holy Ghost, for evermore.

(*Charles Coffin, trs John Chandler*)

PRAYER SUBJECT   *United Nations peace keepers.*

The Greatest

1 Corinthians 13:8–13

'And now these three remain: faith, resumehope and love. But the greatest of these is love' (v. 13, NIV).

Because the Corinthians were at variance with each other their effectiveness was reduced, and their fellowship impoverished. They had rich and varied gifts which should have ensured a massive success in ministry both to the ungodly and to each other, but love, that essential ingredient, was lacking. The absence of love damaged them as individuals (*v. 2*) and their achievements gained them nothing either (*v. 3*).

The drift from a gospel of grace was as evident in the Corinthians as it was with the Galatians (*Gal 3:1–14*) and as it is sometimes with us. There seems to be a residual element in human hearts which persuades us that we can merit the favour of God whereas, quite clearly, we cannot (*Rom 1:16,17*). The gospel is good news because it is a gospel of love; not gifts and work, or even faith and hope. Love is all-inclusive because all people can love and be loved. Ability, potential, education, social class and culture can divide and exclude people, but love, and love alone, has the power to include everyone.

To the Corinthians, Paul emphasised the obvious that love is supreme in this life and the life to come. Love is greater even than faith and hope, because they can exist without love, but the love of which Paul wrote cannot exist without faith or hope.

It is appropriate that we conclude this magnificent hymn on the subject of love as we commence our meditations on the Incarnation of our Lord. The apostle John wrote, 'For God so loved the world that he gave his one and only Son, that whoever believes in him shall not perish, but have eternal life' (*John 3:16*). Christ was born to us as the embodiment of God's love.

PRAYER
> *Love came down at Christmas,*
> *Love all lovely, love divine;*
> *Love was born at Christmas,*
> *Star and angels gave the sign.*

(*Christina Georgina Rossetti*)

Joseph

Matthew 1:18–24

'This is how the birth of Jesus Christ came about: His mother Mary was pledged to be married to Joseph' (v. 18a, NIV).

The spotlight in nativity plays is almost always focused on Mary but usually the circle of light manages to encompass the boy, or man, who plays the part of Joseph. We are used to the idea that Mary was carefully chosen to be the mother of our Lord, she being the 'highly favoured' of the Lord (*Luke 1:28*). Even so, and without detracting from the significance of Mary, a few moments of meditation would persuade us that Joseph, also, was favoured and specially selected for his role. It could be argued that Joseph's contribution was to provide Jesus with the lineage of King David, thereby fulfilling the ancient prophecies (*Isa 11:5*), but there was much more to Joseph than that.

That the house of David had fallen on hard times is shown by the fact that, instead of being cossetted as a royal person, Joseph earned his living as a village carpenter (*13:55*). In God's strategy, however, that was a distinct advantage insofar as it enabled Jesus to grow up in an ordinary home with which people could identify, rather than a palace, but Joseph belonged to David's city, Bethlehem, and that enabled another prophecy to be fulfilled (*Micah 5:2*). Joseph, however, was a man well fitted for his distinct place in history.

When a Jewish couple was pledged, or betrothed to each other, it was recognised as the stage before marriage. The relationship bound them together and could only be broken by death or divorce. When Joseph learned of Mary's condition (*v. 18b*), being a righteous man – we note the adjective – and a kind man (we note his intention in *v. 19*), we begin to understand why God chose him as our Lord's earthly father. From a human perspective Joseph was destined to be the role model for God's Son.

TO PONDER   *God chose and carefully prepared*
*   The man who for the Christ would be*
The head of his blest family;
*   The one who worked, the one who cared,*
The father filling well his role
Of nurturing the Saviour's soul.

Joseph – The Right Man

Matthew 1:18–24

'This is how the birth of Jesus Christ came about: His mother Mary was pledged to be married to Joseph' (v. 18a, NIV).

Learning of Mary's pregnancy must have been a great blow to Joseph, and her explanation – we assume that she told of the angel's visit – that she was pregnant by the Holy Spirit must have confounded him. Joseph would have had his dreams for the future and these would not include the shame of a premarital pregnancy. This was the reason why, after careful thought, he decided to divorce Mary 'quietly' (*v. 19*). He was, however, a man of great sensitivity towards God and when the angel confirmed with him that Mary's account was true, Joseph was totally compliant with the divine will (*v. 24*). He made Mary his wife and when the child was born, gave him the name of Jesus.

When the census was decreed by Caesar Augustus, Joseph could have left Mary behind in Nazareth, but that might have exposed her to gossip, and he took her with him (*Luke 2:1–7*). Again, following angelic advice, (*2:13*) Joseph took his family to Egypt to escape Herod and returned to Nazareth when the danger was over (*2:19–23*). He took good care of Mary and the Christ-child.

We know that Joseph was faithful in his temple worship and, although anxious when Jesus was missing on the journey home, there seemed to be more understanding than censure (*Luke 2:41–51*). Having been made aware of the uniqueness of Jesus, we wonder how Joseph felt as he instructed the boy in the carpenter's art. With supreme gentleness, insight and righteousness Joseph helped to shape the character of his eldest son. Jesus would learn his skills as other boys learned theirs (*cf. Luke 2:52*); he would learn, also, how to work with people and how to apply righteousness to the daily task. As we would expect, God made no error when he chose Joseph to be the earthly father of Jesus.

TO PONDER

> *What kind of man*
> *Did God require for his great plan?*
> *A man strong-willed,*
> *By love and righteousness fulfilled;*
> *A man of vision and of common sense*
> *Who found in faithfulness his recompense.*

A Simple Narrative

Matthew 1:20–24

'When Joseph woke up, he did what the angel of the Lord had commanded him and took Mary home as his wife' (v. 24, NIV).

The biblical record concerning the birth of Jesus makes no attempt to romanticise this, the most significant event in world history. Each account is given with an economy of words which serves only to add dignity and restraint to the occasion. There is, for instance, not the slightest suggestion of the discomfort and hardship involved for Mary and Joseph as they travelled from Nazareth to Bethlehem; no complaint regarding the accommodation they found, the life-threatening lack of facilities and apparent absence of support. Above and around this dramatic and undramatised happening, there is an atmosphere of complete trust, the divine providence and a glorious destiny.

Largely, because of Luke's more detailed account, we feel as though we know Mary, but Joseph remains relatively unknown and it is only by looking at the task he was called upon to do, and by making assumptions from his performance, that his character begins to emerge. Obviously, a strong, resourceful, obedient and godly man was needed to enable the planned Incarnation to proceed without hindrance, and the Scriptures reveal that Joseph was that kind of man. A lesser man simply would not do.

We take note of the decisive responses Joseph made to the angel's guidance. He did not hesitate, argue, rationalise or consider other options but got on with the task. Neither did he count the cost. It seemed as though his home and carpenter's shop in Nazareth were worth little or nothing to him compared with the enormous value of the Christ-child. The glad acceptance and obedience to God shown by Mary was equalled by the obedience of Joseph. As head of the household, protector, provider and mentor, Joseph proved God's choice to be correct.

PRAYER
> Not many, Lord, could do as Joseph did,
> Fulfilling that unique and marvellous role,
> Of making sure the infant Christ was hid
> From those who made his death their supreme goal.
> But in our own and less dramatic way,
> We too can prove our worth as we obey.

Christmas Eve

Luke 2:1–7

'While they were there, the time came for the baby to be born'
(v. 6, NIV).

The long journey from Nazareth was over and the disappointment
regarding accommodation put into perspective as Joseph and Mary
waited in the stable – or perhaps it was a cave – for the child to be born.
Those of us who have been nurtured in Christianity know that the
makeshift birthing-room has been sanitised by the charm of dozens of
nativity plays. And the paintings or cut-outs of animals have turned the
original occupants of the stable into reverent, awe-struck witnesses of
the world's greatest night. The same nativity plays have given us a picture
of Joseph and Mary patiently awaiting the visit of the shepherds (*vv. 8–
20*) and the homage of the wise men (*Matt 2:1–11*).

We accept our stylised presentations of the birth of Jesus without
much difficulty, but the reality would have been quite different.
Improvisation must have been a major requirement on Christmas Eve
and who, we wonder, assisted at the birth? Were there women who came
from the inn to deliver the child – or was Jesus delivered by Joseph? We
do not know and the Bible does not tell us, but there would be
apprehension and pain before there was peace and pleasure, in that less-
than-adequate birth place.

One of Joseph's duties was to name the child, although the name was
already known to Mary (*Luke 1:31*). As he waited for the birth, giving
encouragement and assistance to Mary, we imagine him fulfilling this
task. 'She will give birth to a son,' said the angel, 'and you are to give
him the name Jesus, because he will save his people from their sins'
(*Matt 1:21*). During the months leading up to this time, Mary and Joseph
would have talked of the angel's visits. They would have talked of God's
timing and the greatness of the need, and now the time was at hand, the
stage was set, the Christ would soon be born.

PRAISE   *The pain of birth would soon give way to joy,*
          Tomorrow would the Son of God be born;
        The world's great need awaited this pure boy,
          Whose birthday meant our day of hope would dawn.
        All those who looked to him would freedom find,
        And share the joys God planned for all mankind.

The Infant Christ

Luke 2:1–7

'She gave birth to her firstborn, a son' (v. 7, NIV).

On this day of world-wide excitement with the opening of presents, singing of carols, families coming together and special church services, we celebrate the birth of our Lord. Of his coming the apostle John wrote, 'The Word became flesh and made his dwelling among us' (*John 1:14*) but Joseph, appointed by God to be the earthly father of Jesus, probably did not have John's profound theological statement running through his mind as he looked down at the child so painfully and recently born. More probably, Joseph, having given the divinely chosen name (*Matt 1:21*) to Jesus, was thinking that this very special child looked much the same any other newly-born baby.

Although Joseph was aware of Jesus's destiny he could see he was a child, a baby needing food and care, who needed to be comforted, to feel his mother there. A child who smiled and gurgled, slept and woke, and through whose sparkling eyes a world of mercy spoke. The dimly-lit stable would glow even brighter with Heaven's light when the shepherds arrived to tell their story (*vv. 8–20*), and brighter still when the wise men from the East arrived (*Matt 2:1–11*), adding their confirmation that the world's day of deliverance had arrived.

PRAISE

The infant child who in that manger lay
With all the weakness, helplessness of birth,
Was heralding the dawn of that new day
Long promised for our sad and hopeless earth.
The knowledge of his nature was confined
To but a few who had God's confidence,
A chosen few who shared his love and mind,
Who him obeyed, and showed him reverence.

It takes much insight, and much faith to see
The mind, the heart of God in that small frame;
To see that he who is Divinity
Had taken human form and human name.

And yet, how else could God himself reveal,
Except through flesh, to make his nature real?

The Infant Saviour

Matthew 1:20–24

'She will give birth to a son, and you are to give him the name of Jesus, because he will save his people from their sins' (v. 21, NIV).

Our Lord's birth in a stable to a working-class couple enables the vast majority of people across the world to identify with him. Not unreasonably, the wise men expected him to be born in a palace. Our expectations would have been the same: where else should a royal prince be born? God, however, had a strategy which far exceeded human thought. The name Jesus has come to us through the Latin and Greek forms of the Hebrew name of Jeshua or Joshua. This means God is Salvation and speaks of our Lord's prime mission. He has come to save his people.

Looking down at the infant cradled in his mother's arms Joseph could not have imagined the scope and immensity of the undertaking for which Jesus had been born. Nazareth was not Israel's finest city (*John 1:46*) and there would be much there to persuade Joseph that a Saviour was needed, but Mary's child, the child committed to his care, was to be the Saviour of the entire world. How desperately the world needed a Saviour then, and how desperately we need a Saviour today!

PRAISE   *And is this infant-child a Saviour too?*
    Will those small hands, now weak and lightly curled
In God's time Satan's evil web undo,
    And carry all the sins of all the world?
A child he lies, his brow untroubled now,
    Dependent, as all little children are,
Although one day sharp thorns will pierce his brow
    But that dark day lies in the distance far.

This child is Saviour! Come to fill that role;
    Born of our flesh with us to identify.
On life's hard pathway pure will be his soul,
    And by life's pathway, he for all will die.

The crib and thorn-crown – each to each belong –
Like Calvary's triumph and the angel song.

PRAYER SUBJECT   *Homeless and destitute people*

The Infant King

Matthew 1:20–24

'Joseph son of David, do not be afraid' (v. 20b, NIV).

The Old Testament contains many prophecies which are known as Messianic promises. Some of these prophecies are much used during Advent and refer to Christ as the coming king – a king of the line of Jesse or David. The Messiah is to be a Branch from the root of Jesse (*Isa 11:1; cf. Jer 23:5; 33:15,16*). He is to be a king who will come from Bethlehem (*Micah 5:2*); he will be a king coming to Jerusalem 'gentle and riding on a donkey' (*Zech 9:9*). Joseph, the carpenter of Nazareth but more importantly son of David, was the human means through whom these prophecies were fulfilled. Some scholars say that Mary was also of David's line, but that is difficult to prove and is not important.

God has never been slow to use humble people to achieve his purposes and Joseph, although David's blood coursed through his veins, was a humble man. He had some of the courage of David, and much of his faith. He combined also those qualities of high and low status which enabled him to fulfil the prophecies, and possess the contact with ordinary people which was essential to Christ's upbringing. Did Joseph, we wonder, as he looked at the infant Jesus realise he was looking at his King?

TO PONDER

This helpless child, can he be Heaven's King,
*   Has he surrendered Heaven and Heaven's throne?*
Is this the one of whom the angels sing,
*   Who, out of love will make mankind his own?*

What majesty and might did he forsake,
*   Our evil world to enter and to share?*
What other sacrifices did he make
*   To prove mankind was still within God's care?*

This child, soft-cradled in the arms of love,
*   Exposed and yet protected by God's might*
Would soon, in this our world of darkness, prove
*   He is our only way, our life and light.*

'Behold your King' – so speak his mother's eyes,
'The King who is of faith and love the prize.'

The Infant God

Matthew 1:20–24

'Joseph, son of David, do not be afraid to take Mary home as your wife, because what is conceived in her is from the Holy Spirit' (v. 20, NIV).

When God decided that his Son would come into our world in human form, he virtually decreed that we would have to come to terms with certain mysteries. In one sense, if Jesus had come as a super-terrestrial visitor displaying god-like powers, it might have been easier for mankind to accept him, but God chose the more effective although more mysterious way. Our key verse indicates part of the mystery, but God's chosen method ensured that Jesus was born of woman, and became part of a human family.

In the Gospels, the claim is made that Jesus is uniquely the Son of God, as one of our most familiar verses makes clear, 'God so loved the world that he gave his one and only Son' (*John 3:16*). We add to that the fact that Jesus claimed to be the Son of God (*John 8:34ff*). But there is more to this mystery than that, many of us feel – as did many people then – that Jesus can be understood properly only when we regard him as the Son of God. Attempts to explain him otherwise always leave out one vital factor or another. This means, of course, that as Joseph and Mary looked at Jesus, they were looking at the God-child.

PRAISE

And is he God, this soundly sleeping child?
  Is it conceivable that God could shed
Transcendent power, and share with men defiled
  A world with evil and un-faith o'erspread?

How could God, with this child's contentment, say
  That he is willing here on earth to dwell,
Exchanging Heaven's sublime, continuing day,
  For people and for cultures which rebel?

But if he is God's Son, and Son of Man,
  Of God's own essence, and of man's own flesh,
Then God has made, and shown his master-plan
  Whereby a fallen world can start afresh.

O sleeping child, O Son of God most high –
Fulfil our dreams, and our hopes satisfy.

Towards the Millennium

Psalm 90:1–6

'For a thousand years in your sight are like a day that has just gone by, or like a watch in the night' (v. 4, NIV).

Our celebrations of the birth of Jesus this year lead us into the celebration of the Millennium. Those parts of the world which follow the Western Calendar, the calendar which treats the birth of Jesus as a dividing line in history, have been seeking original ways of celebrating the two thousand years since our Lord's birth. Not every celebration will meet our approval; the leisure industry's ability to exploit every opportunity to capitalise on events appals us. But we, who are Christ's, plan to celebrate this anniversary of the Incarnation properly.

Heaven, of course, has seen millennia come and go and, in one sense, they must be inconsequential. As the Psalmist said, 'a thousand years in your sight are like a day that has just gone by, or like a watch in the night'. Two thousand of our years by the first reckoning is, at most, two days in Heaven's time or even, by the second reckoning of a four-hour night-watch, would pass like the briefest of eight hours.

God, however, is not treating this celebration of the millennium unconcernedly. He knows our human way of using birthdays, anniversaries and the new year as occasions to reflect on what we have done with the past, and how we can improve the future. Our willingness to be awed by history and relate ourselves to it positively is well known to him. With the special emphases this millennium is making, there will be many people who – perhaps not for the first time – will reflect upon the meaning of life, and come to the conclusion that the Christ whose birth we have just celebrated, and propose to celebrate even more, is the only one who can make life meaningful for them. Through his Spirit, God is going to achieve much in the next few days.

PRAYER
Lord, let this time of celebration
Be for some a time of grace;
A time of thoughtful meditation
When, in hope, they seek your face.
And by your Spirit help the needy come
To find new life in this millennium.

The Eternal Christ

Hebrews 13:8

'Jesus Christ is the same yesterday and today and for ever' (v. 8, NIV).

Part of the emphasis of the millennium relates to the passage of time because it is two thousand years since Christ was born. Although other emphases are being made the accent should be on time leading to eternity. Human history may see another millennium but we will not, since our time on earth is limited. Furthermore, no one can forecast what society will be like in a hundred years' time because of the rapid developments being made in technology, and any forecast for the thousand years to come would be pointless. There are, however, certainties to which we can point and to which future generations can cling.

Those certainties are encapsulated in our key verse. Of this verse T.H. Robinson wrote, 'This is one of the greatest single sentences in the New Testament. Adequate comment upon it would involve a complete history of the Christian Church, especially of its inner life, and a prospect of the whole of the spiritual future of mankind.' Because of this, our selected verse is perfectly suitable for our millennium meditations.

As Jesus is unchanging, so are the Father and the Holy Spirit and in our rapidly changing world we need this assurance. Our consumer-orientated society has accustomed us to items once considered crucial now being unobtainable because of the march of progress. It would be terrible indeed if, burdened by our guilt in this generation, where guilt is increasingly unfashionable, we sought God's forgiveness only to hear a recorded voice say, 'We are sorry but, because of changing trends in society, forgiveness is no longer obtainable'! That deep and desperate need of the honest, heavy-laden heart needs a response from the Saviour and, because he is the same today as when he was crucified for the sins of the world, he responds with forgiveness.

PRAYER

And art thou not the Saviour still,
*   In every place and age the same?*
Hast thou forgot thy gracious skill,
*   Or lost the virtue of thy name?*

(*Charles Wesley*)

The Eternal Resource

Hebrews 13:8

'Jesus Christ is the same yesterday and today and for ever' (v. 8, NIV).

On this last day of the old millennium we celebrate the victories of Christ. Two thousand years ago God laid his child in the bosom of a Jewish maiden, promising 'He will be great and will be called the Son of the Most High' and that 'his kingdom will never end' (*Luke 1:31–33*). Mary and Joseph may well have cherished thoughts of Jesus's success, but no one could have imagined the amazing impact of his person, ministry and Kingdom.

Across the world and down the centuries, because Jesus has remained the same – life-giving, prayer-answering and hope-fulfilling – the most adventurous projects have been undertaken in his name. Ordinary people, moved to 'expect great things from God' and 'attempt great things for God' have succeeded beyond their wildest dreams. The gospel has been tested under the most demanding conditions and has not failed. Lives have been changed and communities, even nations, have yielded to the power of the Holy Spirit. If 'yesterday' is intended to cover the period from our Lord's redemptive death to this present moment, Christian history confirms the claim that Christ is the same.

As we look back over our own yesterdays – and we do so without undue pride because some of our shortcomings have dismayed us – we have confidence because we know that sins, once confessed are covered by his forgiveness. We know, also, that those wilful, foolish actions which we long to withdraw but cannot, are subject to his creative, remedial skills. Only the Christ, who made something wonderful out of a Matthew, Zaccheus, Simon the Zealot, Mary Magdalene, Saul of Tarsus and millions of others in this past two thousand years, can do something for us. We come, therefore, to the end of this millennium in humility but in confidence. He is the same yesterday and today. Hallelujah!

PRAISE

> *All the promises of Jesus*
> *Are unchanged in every way,*
> *In my yesterdays I proved them,*
> *I believe them for today.*

(John Gowans, SASB 324)

INDEX

(as from: Pentecost 1994)

NB. Selected Scripture passages are used for the extended coverage given to each of the great Christian festivals from which each separate volume takes its name. Sundays and the New Year are also given separate treatment, too varied to be included in a general index.